JANE AUSTEN'S AUNT
BEHIND BARS

T0284540

JANE AUSTEN'S AUNT BEHIND BARS

Writers and Their Criminal Relatives and Associates, 1700–1900

Stephen Wade

THAMES RIVER PRESS

Jane Austen's Aunt Behind Bars

THAMES RIVER PRESS
An imprint of Wimbledon Publishing Company Limited (WPC)
Another imprint of WPC is Anthem Press (www.anthempress.com)
First published in the United Kingdom in 2013 by
THAMES RIVER PRESS
75–76 Blackfriars Road
London SE1 8HA

www.thamesriverpress.com

A CIP record for this book is available from the British Library.

ISBN 978-0-85728-202-6

Cover design by Sylwia Palka

This title is also available as an eBook

CONTENTS

INTRODUCTION

In 2011, poet Ayat Al-Qurmezi was sentenced to a year in prison in Bahrain for taking part in illegal protests and for writing a poem which mocked the Sunni rulers. She was later pardoned, but the case illustrates the situation in cultures outside Britain in which literature gives offence in a political or ideological context. If we go back a few centuries, such cases were common in Britain, in the days when sedition was a dangerous act to indulge in, and a prison cell awaited the culprit. Nothing quite gives the impact of cultural differences with regard to freedom and tolerance as the use of prison in a society; the reasons we imprison people reflect our belief system, and a look into the past opens up not only ideologies, but also fears and even paranoia, in past societies.

Writers should, in theory, welcome a spell inside the prison walls: after all, a cell is an excellent place to write and work hard in order to meet a deadline. Distractions are few: a pause for food may be the only interruption in a writing day. In the modern prison, there are showers, daily papers, tea and coffee available, classes in the education department and the opportunity for interesting conversation if the cell-mate is articulate and has some sensitivity to a scribbler's needs. Of course luck is involved. The writer may acquire the pad-mate from hell who blasts out his radio all day, has personal hygiene issues and suffers from verbal diarrhoea. However, every encouragement is given today to prisoners who show enterprise, creativity and panache in their apparent effort to be rehabilitated. There may even be a writer in residence, supplied by the Writers in Prison Network, to help with editing and supply feedback.

But in past times, the sensitive poet or the gentle literary essayist has looked upon the prison bars with horror. Prisons used to be workhouses with the treadmill and the crank; the lash was used, and the chaplain would be constantly bothering the individual with lectures on the unacceptable state of his or her soul. Any creative character would be exhausted by the end of a prison day, having spent hours picking oakum, lifting shot or winding the crank; there would be no energy left for writing, one might think. Yet in spite of these negative thoughts the records show that prisons and creative writing have a long and fruitful relationship in British culture. Even when writers themselves may never have stood in the dock and been sentenced to a period of time 'inside,' they may have known jailbirds and crooks. Indeed, several great writers in Britain were inspired and sustained imaginatively by the experiences of friends and acquaintances who had served time, or 'done some bird.' Dickens is the obvious example: his father John knew the inside of a debtors' prison, and naturally his son took a profound interest in that unpleasant period of his family history.

Outside Britain, the literature of other parts of the world provides ample evidence of the place of prison experience in the richness of the canon of great writers. Novelists, dramatists and poets from François Villon to Dostoievski and from Chekhov to Gramsci have known prisons and been moved to write in them or about them. Many great classic works are concerned with prisons: *For the Term of his Natural Life*, *The Count of Monte Cristo*, *A Day in the Life of Ivan Denisovich*, *The Enormous Room*, *In Cold Blood*, to name but a few. Jail diaries have been written by political prisoners from Michael Davitt to Nelson Mandela. Even Jeffrey Archer was moved to write his prison memories even though he was not thrown into solitary confinement or battered by bullies on the wing. Some writers led lives that related somewhat to that of a prisoner: Michel de Montaigne was arrested and put into the Bastille in 1588, destined to be a hostage, but was released the same day when Catherine de Medici intervened. Maybe he would not have minded a few months in there; after all, he chose a life of bookish leisure over a life embroiled in business affairs.

What follows is a contribution to the story of prison literature in England. I have limited my essays to the period c. 1700–1900 for reasons related to the ideological and political contexts, although the legal material will also be relevant. Also, there exists already a massive literature in-print concerning the penal sufferings of writers in the repressive Tudor period. Few of the people featuring in my book have actually committed criminal acts of a petty, everyday nature themselves: perhaps George Gissing is the best example of this. Most were either friends or relatives in such cases. However, some of the stories are concerned with the relationship between creativity, sensibility and the criminal justice system of the time. Obviously, in most cases, the imprisonment is harsh and includes little time to be creative. But at least for the writers in debtors' prisons in the Georgian years there were facilities which allowed prisoners to have their families with them, as well as access to pen and ink. These were amongst other small luxuries, as they languished, in the hope that their creditors would one day agree to some kind of compromise or until finances came from some source such as a bequest. There were, despite the harshness of the time, a number of philanthropists who cared about the consequences of a world-view which saw prison simply as a place of oblivion.

In other words, prison as a version of purgatory, a period of waiting, suspension in a place one step out of normal life, does allow room for writing or other creative arts. The people chosen as my subjects have mostly had the possibility of doing something useful in their cells or rooms; many of them were not criminal in the sense of having committed an actual criminal offence. Some merely felt drawn to the lives of prisoners, such as Churton Collins, the scholar who took a profound interest in crime and visited criminals in their cells. Many, of course, committed offences which today would not be seen as crimes at all.

The first name that came to mind was Henry Fielding, novelist and magistrate. His 'criminal associates' were too many to mention, as he was working at Bow Street in London, along with his blind brother John, and belongs largely to the mainstream of crime history than to any specific biographical examination of a criminal associate. And yet at the same time he is arguably the one writer in my designated period who knew criminals first-hand and possessed insights of professional knowledge which resulted in him being appointed a Justice of the Peace for Middlesex and Westminster in 1748. It was a post that few would have envied. As his Victorian biographer Frederick Lawrence explains,

> According to the popular notion, his worship generally realised a large income by mulching rich offenders, whilst he upheld the terrors of his office by sending the poor ones to Bridewell or to Newgate. The nick-name conferred on him – that of a trading justice – expressed the character of his office.

But he served with distinction. He explained his situation with regard to this work in a preface to another work:

> I will confess that my private affairs, at the beginning of the winter of 1753 had but a gloomy aspect; for I had not plundered the public or the poor of those sums which men, who are always ready to plunder both as much as they can, have been pleased to suspect me of taking…

In other words, he performed the duties with probity and a sense of morality and fairness.

What do I hope to achieve in these essays? Mainly, I aim to explore and explain prison as a significant part of the lives of certain writers – a part that somehow enriched, influenced or enhanced the creative lives of those in focus. After all, prison just as a metaphor is a rich source of inspiration and always has been: Sir Walter Raleigh took this to extremes when he wrote, 'the world itself is but a large prison, out of which some are daily led to execution' as he returned to prison after his trial. What becomes a powerful force for sustenance and strength when 'inside' is the feeling that freedom is an illusion wherever one happens to be – a sentiment which naturally requires a degree of stoicism and resolve.

There is also the matter of the shock of incarceration; on the face of it, the central theme of my book is that of sensitive souls suddenly confronted by the terrors of being locked in a confined space, totally subjugated to the will of others, trapped in the lower depths of the criminal justice system. But such experience is not that simple. For much of the Georgian years, although the terror of prison was rife, the worst threat came from gaol fever, not the thought of violence or confinement *per se*. At that time, prisons were not, for the most part, a punishment, but rather a place for detention until trial or until release when financial circumstances changed. When they began to be thought of as houses of industry, and houses of correction were established, then matters changed.

In British prisons, Newgate stands out as a place related to writers and poets; not only has it housed hundreds of scribblers, but it has also spawned the famous *Newgate Calendar*: stories of criminals issued at various times between the late eighteenth and early nineteenth century. This compendium of tales from the gaol includes biographies covering the whole spectrum of criminals from pirates to fraudsters and from robbers to killers. Many of the inmates of Newgate over the years have been writers, going back to the fifteenth century, when Sir Thomas Malory was locked up there, no doubt working on his *Morte D'Arthur*. The prison reached mythic status in John Gay's hugely successful *Beggar's Opera* of 1728. But in more recent years, other prisons across the land have had their writers, from Jeffrey Archer in Belmarsh and Lincoln to Charles Bronson, in virtually every prison within the system.

Looking through the pages of history, down into the chronicles of literature and of writers' lives, it soon becomes apparent that writing is inevitably subversive, and that writers have offended the authorities for all kinds of reasons. With a multiplicity of offences on the statute books in Georgian Britain in particular, it was not so difficult to cross the line into criminal activity. A great deal of English literature is run through with dissent of some kind that challenges ideology, philosophical grounds of law and indeed the very regime in which the authors lived. The case of the Chartists illustrates this most clearly. Many of these were working men or artisans, men who were self-taught and infused with a spirit of improvement; their beliefs in political change often sprang from social inequality, and of course, in their writings they described the malaise of their time.

Even today, when the prison population is around 86,000 (January 2013) and cell blocks are packed, writing is seen as one of the strands of self-development which may help in the rehabilitation of offenders, along with drama, art and storytelling. But we live in adventurous and innovative times in our penology; in the nineteenth century the only approved books inside were the Bible and religious tracts, and creative writing was unknown, although many middle-class prisoners indulged in exactly that, as my chapters will demonstrate.

Most interestingly of all, my tales of writers inside will highlight some of the less well-known aspects of their related biographies, of both the criminals themselves and of the writers who knew them. Perhaps one of the most significant spin-off elements of the writers' lives in the following pages is exemplified by the circle around Conan Doyle and the beginnings of the Crimes Club. Here is the genesis of that sub-culture of literary men (it tends to be mostly male) that mixes literature and the study of crime. Their lives illustrate clearly what the parallels are: both writing and criminal lives have that quality of mystery mixed with artistic prowess, and both are riddled with teasing questions of motive. Thomas de Quincey had his tongue in his cheek when he wrote his famous mock-lecture on *Murder Considered as one of the Fine Arts* in 1827, treating the subject as something worthy of serious attention by scholars, while at the same time offering a critique of the genre we now know as true crime. In the twentieth century, such aspects of the lives of amateur criminologists have flowered in all kinds of ways, from the respect given to memoirs by prisoners, lawyers and policemen, to the documentary presentation of crime topics on film or radio.

In spite of all these general considerations, the following essays are concerned primarily with prison and crime as experienced either by the writers themselves or by their friends and relatives. I have only distorted the perspective on one occasion, the sad story of Mary Lamb – although she experienced no prison walls as such, her home became one, with her brother Charles as keeper. I have included this because it involves a highly unusual process of law within the criminal justice system at the time. Otherwise, I remain concerned with criminal offences, cells and rooms within prison walls, as well as dramas in court.

It is certainly not difficult to find writers across the years that have been in trouble with the law, and their encounters with the consequences of various transgressions sometimes make for harrowing reading. Yet some of the most fascinating stories entail offences and moral outrage that open up particular insights into the society of the time. For instance, Émile Zola, after defending the unfortunate Dreyfus in one of France's greatest scandals concerning a dreadful miscarriage of justice, became a celebrity, but in England, his publisher, Henry Vizetelly, ended up in prison for corrupting public morals. Often, the writer concerned has a life of sheer want and desperation, as in the case of playwright Philip Massinger, who shared a cell in the Clink Prison with two other writers in 1613, where he begged for a small sum of cash from a producer in order to keep himself sane and fed.

If we look for sheer explicit controversy and something that inextricably ties literature and prison together, there is no better example than the poet Ezra Pound, who wrote *The Pisan Cantos* while in an army detention camp near Pisa. His poetry, ranked by many as some of the best written in the twentieth century, came not only from prison but from a mind clearly riddled with prejudice. He was on a treason charge and found poetry to be his main consolation. And with a mental illness weighing him down, the product was like nothing else in the canon of American poetry.

In terms of sources, the most vivid and memorable has to be the records of the Old Bailey: in those online accounts of court proceedings lies the genesis of my book, because reading the account of the trial of Dr Baretti for murder, I came across the actual words spoken in court by Dr Samuel Johnson. Not only did his character come through, as always, powerful and controlled, but I also felt that the years dividing us had dissolved and I was amongst those watching in the gallery. Such is the potential thrill of looking into the history we all inherit. Other sources include letters and biographies, describing the moments when a writer finds that a relative or a friend is in trouble with the law. In past times when the authorities could come down very hard on transgressors, those sources can be strongly emotional and dramatic too.

Prison and creativity continue to be an area of life very much in focus in the year 2013, when the prisons of the world are bursting with dissidents, nay-sayers, poets, bohemians, wanderers and misfits whose lives and acts do not align with accepted laws and morality. This has always been the case, but in today's world there is a higher level of curiosity surrounding them and their writing, painting or music. Unfortunately, in less enlightened states, this is still not the case and the dark shadow of the noose sheds its misery across many writers in cells for their beliefs. It is valuable to hold that thought as the following essays venture back in time to periods in Britain where punishments for both criminals and debtors were severe, and enlightened thinking hard to find.

Running alongside the biographies, I offer up the stories of various prisons, and of these, Newgate tends to dominate. In the Georgian period it was horrendous, and in 1818 the Grand Jury of the City of London, following other reformers who had been busy trying to improve the penal system for the previous fifty years, wrote to the *Times* and had this to say about the prison:

> The deplorable situation of the male prisoners, with respect to clothing, particularly the juvenile part, made a melancholy impression on our minds. Many were without shoes or stockings, others without shirts, and one almost in a state of nakedness… we are of the opinion that the general health of the prisoners of both sexes would be improved if an allowance of soap was granted…

In contrast, one thing that strikes the historian with regard to literary prisoners is the notable range of differences in prison lifestyle. Leigh Hunt set up home and prison became a haven of domesticity, and William Combe could walk outside until curfew, while in contrast George Gissing was treated like a common thief.

Of course, there is one notable category of offences which is omitted from these pages: suicide. Suicide and attempted suicide were criminal offences in Britain until 1961. Therefore, technically, such literary figures as Thomas Chatterton, who succeeded in taking his own life at the age of seventeen, and Mary Wollstonecraft, who tried to kill herself by plunging into the Thames, could be included in terms of crime, but there was no prison experience for them. The same could be said for participation in duels, notably by playwright Richard Brinsley Sheridan, who fought two duels with Thomas Mathews, and was stabbed in the second encounter, but no criminal proceedings ensued. However, debt, which was the cause of so many spells in gaol, did briefly impinge on his life. He had the huge sum of £28,000 due to him, but had debts and so was arrested; he was very briefly incarcerated but was released after a friend's intervention.

In most instances, the criminals were well away from the writers and 'criminal associates' were incidental in the writer's life. But nevertheless the curiosity is there, and in this sidelight on literary history, Newgate figures prominently yet again. The story of Lady Mary Wortley Montagu perhaps typifies this use of prison and criminals by those in higher echelons of society. In 1723 she wrote to her sister,

> I am sorry to inform you of the death of our nephew my sister Gower's son of the smallpox. I think she has a great deal of reason to regret it, in consideration of the offer I made to her... of taking the child to my house where I would have inoculated him...

There was widespread fear of inoculation, but Lady Mary had experimented, and learned while in Turkey of its use. She was up against extreme prejudice. Many saw inoculation as black magic, and as something that was against God's natural state of things.

Smallpox was rife in the gaols, and in society generally. Lady Mary Wortley Montagu, who was the wife of an English diplomat in

Turkey, was a victim, scarred by its ravages. In England, long before Edward Jenner demonstrated the use of inoculation, she had her own daughter inoculated, and such first steps encouraged medical men of her time to experiment. Some used Newgate prisoners as guinea pigs for such experiments. Charles Maitland introduced the vaccine into England, and he devised the prison tests. The King agreed that the prisoners who consented to have smallpox engrafted on them would be freed if they recovered. The man who actually went into the prison to perform the test was Dr Terry of Enfield, who had worked on similar tests in Turkey.

Inoculations were done on six condemned men and they all recovered. The next stage was that one of the recovered men was sent to Hertford Gaol where it was known that the illness was rife, and there the man was to lie in bed with a sufferer. The prisoner was not affected, which was a great encouragement to the doctors. More trials were then conducted on charity children in the parish of St James. Smallpox was not eradicated until 1977, and it remained a problem in prisons throughout the nineteenth century as well. As late as 1893 there was an outbreak at Hull Prison and at Gateshead Workhouse at the same time.

Of course, in the years of my survey, much of the subject was concerned with status and reputation; a criminal in the nineteenth century entered prison usually as the first step down in a dark, stigmatic descent into a state of non-being. Unless, as some writers did simply as part of a crusade or a stunt, a person moved from the writer's study to a prison cell, then they were lost. Who would want to know them? George Gissing served his time in Manchester and then when in London he was what he wanted to be with the past forgotten and not spoken of. But equally, prison experience was absolutely absorbing to creative souls and the visit to a prison or mental asylum was almost inevitable as creativity and poverty went hand in hand.

Finally, comparing the twentieth century with the two previous ones in this respect proves to be interesting. In a book called *Under Arrest* by Giacomo Papi, we have a history of the twentieth century in mug shots. Of the 174 subjects, only five are writers: the proportions have declined, or perhaps, far more likely, the writers have kept their heads down except in those states in which repression is now as it once was for Britain, in these tempestuous Georgian and Victorian years.

One outstanding line of thought emerges when we compare the nineteenth century situation with regard to writers and prison experience: prison life today is familiar to us through media and the literature from the prisoners themselves is easy to obtain. The mystique of incarceration has virtually disappeared and our hunger for more and more daring, intrusive and shocking documentary narratives on prison life, while still there, is more fully met by access to what was previously arcane knowledge. One reason for this is, naturally, the end of capital punishment and the loss of the horrendous ritual of judicial killing.

A consequence of this has been the emergence of that branch of the true crime genre written by prisoners and indeed prison staff; one might argue that this is merely a continuation of the Georgian narratives written by the 'ordinaries' (chaplains) attending condemned persons, but of course, a literary version of this literature has emerged, so that the experience of prison life, from all perspectives, has been opened up to the general reader with much more richness and diversity than previously. The writers are still entering the prison walls, but some of them are wearing uniforms or making legal visits: the monopoly of prison literature held by the inmates is being challenged. The contrasts between prison experience today and Victorian prison life are sharper than ever and creative writing is opening up the regimes for inspection.

THE CONTEXT

CRIME AND PUNISHMENT 1700–1900

What kind of criminal justice system did the writers in my biographies live within? The following is an overview, to help place the stories in their time. In terms of the destinations of my subjects, the system was such that it offered alternatives to prison – service in the army, asylums or transportation (the latter still being a prison sentence, but with a long period out of a cell and work in the open air).

When we think of the popular images of crime in the 'long' eighteenth century (c. 1700–1837), the aspects of the period that come to mind are probably Dick Turpin the highwayman, desperate and ruthless smugglers and horrible hangings at Tyburn. These kinds of images stem partly from popular culture – mainly film and novels – but also from countless illustrations in books, magazines and documentaries depicting the sheer vicious lawlessness of that century. The myths were perpetuated by popular fiction, such as Harrison Ainsworth's novel, *Rookwood*, and by the ballads sold on the streets.

In fact the most dominant criminal events of those years were arguably the Jacobite insurrections of 1715 and 1745; the riots and disorder which occurred for all kinds of reasons: offences against the Game Laws, transportation, the birth of professional police, and sedition. Although there was a high level of homicide and crimes against the person during this period, along with a series of repressive murder acts, what takes the limelight in crime history is the political narrative.

If we look at some of the major legislation of the time, we find a hugely influential statute in 1715, The Riot Act; then the 1718 Transportation Act, which gave courts the power to transport felons to the American colonies; the Black Act of 1723 which added a large number of offences to the established 'Bloody Code,' the name given to the brutal series of statutes through the eighteenth century, and finally the various acts against sedition and radicalism in the Regency years. These all aimed at preventing the open or secret dissemination of radical political ideas during and after the French Revolution of 1789.

Violence and Fear

The period is marked at every level of crime as one of horrendous repression and punishment. The British citizen was under threat from robbers and muggers at all times in the towns and of course in London, but nocturnal fears were severe: after all, a man and his household were only protected by the 'watch and ward' officers who were generally ineffective. By the Regency years, we have Sir Robert Peel's Police Act of 1829, and much earlier there were the Bow Street magistrates and 'Runners' in London, but for the country in general, there were perils everywhere.

In 1728, for instance, John Byrom had a meeting with a highwayman. He wrote a letter to his wife describing this:

> ...within about half a mile or less of Epping, a highwayman in a red rug upon a black horse came out of the bushes up to the coach, and presenting pistol, first at the coachman and then at the corporation within, with a volley of oaths demanded our money...

Shots were fired and the passengers parted with cash and silver. The robberies went on daily: copies of the *Gentleman's Magazine* and the *Annual Register* are peppered with reports of nasty and violent attacks, dreadful murders and brutal hangings.

The number of capital crimes gradually increased throughout the Georgian years, and by the 1820s there were over two hundred such offences. Judges on the assize circuits found a procession of culprits standing before them – often very young – who could technically be hanged for what we would think of as small thefts. For a 'grand larceny' the sentence was death, so courts and the bench often humanely changed the value of stolen goods so that offences would be relegated to simple larceny.

A typical example of a crime of this time, when the country was still predominantly rural, is from Lincolnshire in 1760, when Mary Baker prosecuted a shepherd of Willoughton for assault: he was in court for 'violently beating and abusing her with his foot and for striking her with his fist, and punching her down and striking her head against a wall…' By modern standards, his prison sentence was light: merely six months. But the point is that these attacks were everyday matters.

Riot and Disorder

It was also a time when there was trouble in the streets, in the country, and in the new mills. In 1769 attacks on mills were included in the offences subject to the Riot Act, and later in this period, political radicalism brought extreme measures. In 1799 and 1800 the Combination Acts outlawed meetings in streets of more than six people. After the Luddite troubles of 1812, when machine-wreckers (named after a fabled figure called Ned Ludd) set about destroying mills in Yorkshire, a new offence of administering an illegal oath was created, so that more felons could be hanged or sent to Van Dieman's Land (Tasmania).

Some riots were not merely in response to the price of corn; the Gordon Riots of 1780 in London lasted for six days after Lord George Gordon presented a petition to parliament against Catholic rights. People were killed and in the end 135 people stood trial. Riots were linked to sedition, and in 1792 there was a proclamation against seditious publications, and even the great statesman Thomas Paine was tried *in absentia* and convicted of sedition.

Another aspect of this was mutiny. The Napoleonic Wars led to numerous side-effects, and mutiny was one of these: in 1797 after a dangerous mutiny at the Nore, men were tried and hanged, and in 1819 the assembly of people for political reasons received its most brutal response from the authorities in these years when the Peterloo Massacre occurred in Manchester. It was here that the famous speaker Henry 'Orator' Hunt addressed an immense crowd, gathered peaceably, but the yeomanry intervened and in that bloody encounter, eleven people were killed and many more wounded.

But riots could break out for all kinds of reasons: there were food riots in Cornwall in 1727; anti-enclosure riots in the Forest of Dean in 1735, and election riots in several places in 1734. Crowds gathered to destroy turnpikes in Bristol in 1749 and in 1751 two women suspected of being witches were murdered by a crowd in Tring.

One report in the press from 1755 gives some idea of the trouble that was often experienced:

> May, Selby, Yorks. The bellman made proclamation for the inhabitants to bring their hatchets and axes at 12 o'clock that night to cut down the turnpike erected by Act of Parliament. Accordingly, the great gate with five rails was totally destroyed by some riotous persons...

Tyburn 'Theatre'

The abiding image of the criminal justice system in the Georgian years is one of trials at the Old Bailey and hangings at Newgate or Tyburn, accompanied by huge crowds. Of course, there is some truth to this picture, but we have to remember that while many were sentenced to die, many were reprieved. Between 1814 and 1834 for instance, almost five thousand people were sentenced to hang for burglary, but only 233 were eventually hanged. Even so the hangman was busy. After the Murder Act of 1752, a felon was to be hanged within just 48 hours of sentencing. Until 1760, a 'triple tree' was used at Tyburn: a wooden frame with three sides, so that several people could be hanged at once; this was replaced by a portable gallows in that year.

Hangings at Tyburn (close to Marble Arch) ended in 1783 and from December of that year executions took place at Newgate. The so-called 'new drop' there was the scene of a multiple hanging in 1783, when nine men and a woman were on the scaffold. The masses relished these events of course, with thousands of people swarming the streets to witness the deaths of felons.

Until 1784, a wife who murdered her husband would be burned at the stake rather than hanged, as her crime was petty treason, not murder. In that year Mary Bailey was the last to suffer that horrible fate, although it was common practice for the hangman, for a small bribe, to strangle the women before they were tied to the stake. For treason, a person could be hanged, drawn and quartered, and as late as 1820 this continued, when the famous Cato Street conspirators suffered this fate.

Transportation and Prisons

After the loss of the American colonies, deportation was to Australia, beginning in 1787. Between 1815 and 1829, around 12,000 convicts were transported to Australia. The process involved a period in a specific colony, and then work on probation teams, so that, for instance, convicts in Tasmania would sometimes be allocated to gaols in Richmond and work in teams to do public works, such as bridge-building.

Prisons in this period were seriously dangerous places to be. The assize system meant that prisoners on remand awaiting trial had to languish in disease-ridden cells until the judges arrived on the circuit to clear the gaols. Local gaols and houses of correction were, however, the subject of a study and survey by the great prison reformer John Howard. His book, *The State of the Prisons* (1777) was the first step in the movement towards making prisons more humane and open to some notions of rehabilitation and reform rather than mere punishment and hard work in a 'silent system.'

The eighteenth-century gaol was, however, a mix of factory, punishment block and going concern – in the sense that the wealthier inmates could still have communication with the community outside, buying food and drink and having visitors. Debtors lived alongside hardened criminals: John Wesley's father, Samuel, was a debtor in Lincoln Gaol.

Early Police

This period saw the gradual emergence of the professional police. The brothers Henry and John Fielding had developed a reasonably successful London police force in the mid-century, though its scope was very limited. Then, in 1800, a police office was established in Wapping, and in 1829 the Metropolitan Police Act was passed, forming a paid, full-time force which operated within a radius of about seven miles of London. Provincial forces were to come later.

When Queen Victoria ascended the throne in 1837 there had been significant developments in the criminal justice system, largely thanks to Sir Robert Peel. It would not be stretching the facts too much to say that there had been a revolution in crime and punishment in the ten years before she became queen. Peel had established the first truly professional police force in 1829, and his gaol acts had gone some way to providing regulation and inspection in regional gaols and houses of correction.

The last years of the Regency experienced the widespread fear of political and social change impacting on popular feeling as radicalism had brought massive and often terrifying disorder. But in spite of the riots, sedition and arson of the tough first years of the 1830s, there had been important developments, mainly the abolition of a large number of capital offences. Although the retribution of the courts against criminals was still swift and savage, there were signs that more humane attitudes were coming through. By 1837 only sixteen crimes had capital sentences. The liberal ideologies of the Enlightenment were slowly percolating through society.

By the end of the century, white-collar crime had increased markedly, and serious crime against the person became less prominent. Even so, Britain was still a society with a massive drink problem and violence was never far away, particularly in the new towns where long hours of hard work and deprivation combined with drunkenness created an underclass of so-called 'habitual criminals' who crowded the police courts and magistrates' courts.

A Nation Divided

One notable feature of crime in the first half of Victoria's reign was the acceleration of the class divisions: the rich and poor were sharply aware of their differences. In Manchester in the 1840s for instance, as the novelist Elizabeth Gaskell describes in *North and South*, the villas of the new rich, the masters of industry, were in one area of the city, strictly separate from the urban ghetto in which the mill workers lived in basement slums, struggling with all the problems poverty, poor public health and low wages bring.

In the 1840s, the writers were so aware of what came to be called 'The Two Englands' that it comes as no surprise that the criminal courts were busy. Theft and assault came often from desperation – men stealing to feed the family or women entering the sex trade in order to earn some extra cash.

The Reform Act of 1832 had been a huge disappointment to many of the lower middle class, as so many features of the corrupt and divisive political structures of the land had left them without the vote and other rights. Trade unions were illegal and men were transported or imprisoned for working towards establishing unions. By 1851, the artisan class were beginning to creep into some kind of recognition in a corporate sense, with the creation of the Amalgamated Society of Engineers. But for the working man and woman, most of the Victorian period was one of very long working hours, poor pay and limited social support. The workhouse was a constant threat and was seen as little better than a prison.

Arguably, for the Victorians, the prison itself was simply just another version of a receptacle for the fallen, the lost and the neglected, in a society where material success and wealth meant that many would be pushed to the wall and elbowed out of a life of security and stability.

The Police Reforms

Peel's Metropolitan Police were on the streets by 1829 and by the 1850s, regional forces were being created. There was resistance and suspicion from the start. People thought that a general and professional force would create a police state and they were seen as quasi-military, being compared to the repressive regime in France. After the establishment of the detective force in 1842 these fears were reinforced for many. But the fact is that the new police gradually learned and adapted, so that by the last decades of the century they had specialists to deal with such matters as anarchists, Irish Fenians and large-scale fraud. The C. I. D. was created in 1874 and by the end of the century the top police officers were involved in early measures towards national security.

The 1839 County Police Act gave boroughs the option of starting a constabulary, if the justices wanted to levy a rate for that purpose, and in 1856 the County and Borough Police Act made it compulsory for all counties in England and Wales to establish police forces. In the year of Victoria's accession, the first black police officer was appointed – John Kent, who joined the Carlisle police force.

Tough Punishment

The prison system and the criminal courts still maintained a central ideology of harsh repression and a very narrow, regulatory practice in terms of allowing more of the human element into the justice system. For instance, there was no probation service until 1907, though the police court missionaries did their best to keep offenders out of a recidivist life.

The first model prison was constructed at Millbank. A separate system for men and women was established. A study of the prison plans, published in parliamentary papers, for this period shows the very specific and purpose-built accommodation for different classes and sexes. By 1877 the prisons were effectively nationalized and many old local houses of correction were phased out.

Deportation continued until 1853 to Tasmania (Van Dieman's Land) and in the same year the Penal Servitude Act made the idea of punishment itself, the removal of individual freedom, the core of the penal system. By the 1860s, the application of a ticket of leave process, whereby convicts could be released early for good behaviour, led to epidemics of assaults, notably the garrotting reign of terror on 1863–65 in which gangs preyed on the rich in city streets. The response was, naturally, a call for tougher punishments and more use of the whip and birch. In 1867, deportation ended completely.

By 1861 the number of capital offences was reduced to just four: murder, arson in a royal dockyard, high treason and piracy. In that year the last execution for attempted murder took place when Martin Doyle was hanged in Chester. But public hangings continued until 1868, and up to that time the hanging of a felon was still a public spectacle on a massive scale. In popular culture, murder and hanging were placed in all kinds of narratives and entertainments. Charles Dickens reported that pictures of murderers were in the print shops, and he wrote that 'high prices were offered for murderer's clothes at Newgate.'

Gradually, the public began to see that crime and its growing literature had a harmful side as a bad influence, stressing sensation and violence above any moral worth. At least, that is how many in the establishment saw it and moral responses intensified.

Hangings in a 'Civilized' Society

When we consider the surface features of the Victorian world – polite social events, dances, protocol and good manners – it is easy to forget how barbaric were the acts done in the name of civilization. It may have been a Christian society, but after the 1857 Indian Mutiny for instance, some of the leaders of the rebellion were 'fired at cannon' – meaning that they were strapped across the barrel of a cannon and then obliterated. That was hardly the act of a 'civilized' society and demonstrated only savage repression to the people of India, within the rule of the British imperial ideology.

The same attitudes lay behind the public hangings. In 1840 the murder of Lord William Russell was one of the most notorious Victorian cases: this was because he had been killed by a servant. Until 1829, this offence was classified as petty treason, and the killer would have been burned at the stake, not hanged, as previously mentioned with regard to wives killing husbands. In this case, the killer Francois Courvoisier was hanged. At his trial, crowds pushed and shoved to find a seat at the Old Bailey; the judge presiding was short of room and the name of Courvoisier was on everyone's lips in the taverns and coffee houses. At the hanging there were 40,000 spectators. The novelist, William Thackeray was in the crowd, and he wrote afterwards:

> I came away from Snow Hill that morning with a disgust for murder, but it was for the murder I saw done… So salutary

has the impression of the butchery been upon me that I can see Mr. Ketch at this moment, with an easy air, taking the rope from his pocket…

The hangman was William Calcraft, a celebrity at the time. He had to let the body hang for an hour before he could cut it down. The body was then buried within the walls of Newgate. But just a month after, Courvoisier was seen as a waxwork effigy at Madame Tussaud's.

Courts and Trials

There was a massive amount of legislation throughout the Victorian years affecting the criminal courts. As the century wore on, the police courts took on most of the everyday work, as there was such a high level of petty crime that the magistrates could not cope. But for more serious crime, the assizes and the Old Bailey were the arenas where serious crime would be affected by various developments. In the matter of defences, for instance, both insanity and provocation were extremely hard to prove. The 1843 McNaghten Rules were the main guidance for barristers and judges: Daniel McNaghten at that time tried to murder Sir Robert Peel but was judged to be insane. He was 'labouring under such defect of reason, from disease of the mind, as not to know the nature and the quality of the act he/she was doing.'

For provocation and insanity, there were hundreds of homicide cases in which the killer (usually a husband) tried to claim either 'temporary insanity' because of drunkenness, or provocation because the wife or woman in question was inconstant.

Imprisonment for debts under £20 was abolished in 1844, and in 1861, imprisonment for debt ended completely. But amazingly, it was not until the 1890s that the accused could speak in court and there was also no general court of criminal appeal until 1907. The only chance of a rethink about a criminal court sentence before the end of the century would have been the 'Crown cases Reserved' in which a judge would press the matter in a select group of learned colleagues.

Industrial Relations and Commercial Crime

With the Industrial Revolution and the widespread shift of labour to the new urban conurbations, and the large-scale immigration of workers needed for the new industries, crime came not only with the social divisions and the 'haves and have-nots' but through industrial strife. In terms of industrial problems, the illegality of unions led to constant trouble when 'black-leg' labour was imported. The 1859 Molestation of Workmen Act tried to do something about this but in 1866 the 'Sheffield Outrages' typified the lamentable results of union problems: non-union cutlery workers were attacked by their fellow workmen. In the following year the Master and Servant Act put some limitations on the mechanism for prosecuting strikers for breach of contract but members could still face the law if they were thought to be 'aggravated cases.'

But trouble was always there, ready to erupt. Typical of this was the nine-week strike of cotton weavers in Lancashire in 1878, in which there were confrontations in Preston and Blackburn, along with the celebrated London dockers' strike of 1889 in which the dockers won six pence an hour. In 1893 two people were killed at Featherstone when soldiers and strikers clashed at Acton Hall Colliery.

There was an increase in white-collar crime in the second half of the century, and fraud, forgery and deception were often in the news and reported from the courts. Typical of this was what became known as the first 'true crime' story on film, involving a clerk called Thomas Goudie who forged cheques while working with the Bank of Liverpool. He was threatened by a racetrack gang to do this but was found out and arrested. He was given a sentence of ten years but died in gaol after serving six. Dramatic scenes from Goudie's story were filmed by local filmmakers Mitchell and Kenyon (see *The Lost World of Mitchell and Kenyon*, BBC DVD).

In the City of London, naturally, such crimes proliferated and indeed always did. But recent research has unearthed a number of little-known sources of material on forgery from the Bank of England. A cursory trawl through the London magistrates' courts and the Guildhall, Old Bailey sessions papers and assizes reveal the escalation of fraudulent offences during these years.

The Queen's reign began with trouble in the streets, social divisions and violent domestic crime, and ended with the dominance of counterfeiters, forgers and conmen. The high-profile murders were still there, but the 'crimes of the brain' were stealing the headlines from the muggers and thieves. Naturally, the more literate people in the later nineteenth century, after the growth of elementary education and greater literacy, were involved in fraud and embezzlement, the 'white collar' classification, and writers on the wrong side of the law appear more often at the time, but these tend to be cases involving libel. For instance, we know from the memoirs of some barristers just how many actors, artists and writers were in court in that period, usually for defamation concerning intellectual property law.

1

DEFOE IN NEWGATE AND THE CLINK

Understanding and defining Daniel Defoe is a difficult task. He achieved so many things and lived a life of restless adventure and endeavour, and yet he was very guarded about the interior life and about his private self. In between his exploits, travels and business ventures we get glimpses of him, but on the whole, aspects of his personality elude us. He arguably wrote the first novels in English as we understand that form; he was a government agent; he was a documentary writer; he began countless business concerns, and he rubbed shoulders with all classes of people in society. He could handle danger: when he acted as a spy among the Scots it was during negotiations for the Union of 1707, and it was quite possible that he could have been murdered by a stranger in the street.

He was a Whig and so in favour of the Dutch man who was to be King William III of England; he was crafty and shameless in the art of survival. As George Rosie tells the tale of one of Defoe's poems, he could put on a front, a dissimulation, or as we might say now, he could 'spin' a subject:

> At my Edinburgh secondary school we were taught a poem that used to bring a blush of pride and patriotism to the faces of my sixteen-year-old classmates. It was called *Caledonia, a Poem in Honour of Scotland and the Scots*, and it was written by Daniel Defoe... it had been written by an Englishmen.

In other words, it would appear that he was a chameleon in matters of life and thought. This imposes baffling contradictions on any attempt to understand his life. Who was he really? There have been several biographers, and one thing they all have in common is a notable slice of attention made to Defoe the prisoner.

Daniel Defoe knew many prisons. He knew them as a debtor and as a serious offender. He may be reckoned by many to be the father of the English novel, but in his life, his fiction was only a small fraction of his activities as a constantly busy, enterprising man. He is elusive: biographers often tackle the most elusive subjects; writers, artists and poets often spend so much time on their work that the business of biography is concerned with little else, but in Defoe's case, we have a man who was constantly involved in debate and interplay with the world he knew. That world was the late Stuart and early Georgian Britain, and in that age of chaotic social change when men were apt to rise and fall with equal rapidity, he was in his element. Why did he know prison? He experienced the inside of cells and sponging houses because his business brain and his writing expertise led him into trouble as often as it led him to success.

Before becoming a guest of Her Majesty Queen Anne in Newgate, Defoe knew the inside of a prison as a debtor. In the 1690s he was a married man with a family, working as an entrepreneur in London and elsewhere; he was living at a time when 'projecting' was a way of life for many – those who dreamed of a major investment paying off and settling them in comfort for the rest of their lives. By that time, he was already a veteran of war, having fought for the wrong side in the Monmouth Rebellion of 1685, and his mind was bubbling with plans and ideas as he ventured into both authorship and business. Like many men of his time, he gathered creditors and gradually immersed himself in the murky waters of debt. He tried to fight off disaster by paying small amounts to ward off long-standing creditors, and then invest somewhere else, making major investments. This attitude to business ruined him. The turning point came when he decided to buy some civet cats, as the perfume from their gland secretions was valuable and the market for it was expanding. But he failed in the practicalities of it; even worse, he then invested money belonging to his mother-in-law and lost both affection and trust on his own doorstep. Matters began to involve the law; a man called

Timothy Bird claimed an unpaid debt of £33 (promised to be paid within three months) and Defoe did not deliver. This was a huge sum in 1692.

Defoe had also invested, at the same time, in a diving bell business and that too failed. He was then in deep trouble, as he was served with a subpoena and then, after failing to appear in court, with a commission of rebellion: that meant that should he not go to court, he was an outlaw and the officers were out to grab him. By November 1693 he was in the King's Bench Prison awaiting trial. The situation for bankrupts at that time was horrendously grim: they could languish in prison until debts were sorted out and arrangements made. The amount he owed was a huge, a debt of £17,000 – in modern terms that would be around half a million pounds.

By the seventeenth century the gaols and bridewells (houses of correction) across the land had become places where all kinds of people were crammed together beyond society and left to rot. Only the wealthy, fallen foul of debtors, could enjoy a reasonably comfortable life behind the prison walls, because they could buy food and drink from the traders who came into the prisons. Generally, those dumped into gaols were felons, debtors, small-time thieves, prostitutes, beggars and invalids. They were the last residence of what the society considered to be trash.

On 2 January 1752 an anonymous prisoner wrote this letter to the *Gentleman's Magazine*:

Mr Urban,

I am an unhappy prisoner now lying in one of the gaols within this kingdom, to which I was committed about 10 months past, on an accusation of felony, though entirely innocent as afterwards appeared on my trial, my poverty and want of friends preventing any person till then from speaking the truth in my favour. But the grievance I complain of is not my commitment for a crime of which I was not guilty, but the tyranny and oppression of the gaoler, for after I had been declared innocent by the jury, and the prosecution found to be on malice and ill-nature, instead of being immediately discharged, I was hurried back to the prison again, there to lie till I could raise 30s to pay the gaoler what he calls his fees. If any situation on earth merits pity or any evil merits the attention of the legislature, surely 'tis the case of unhappy prisoners in my circumstances. I have lain here six months, my family starving, my credit and character ruined and my spirits broken, without any means of procuring redress against the unjust prosecutor or any satisfaction for the numerous calamities he has brought upon me. I have heard much talk of the equity of our laws but surely if they had not been defective or abused, I should not now suffer.

The wretched man, in modern terms, had been on remand, guilty of no crime, and yet had been totally ruined in every aspect of his life and health. What we think of as 'remand' at that time was awaiting gaol delivery if at assizes, or some other kind of trial in other courts, and there were dozens of different courts across the land in the Georgian period, from manorial to admiralty and from military to assizes.

Defoe would be in a similar situation: stuck in a limbo among other debtors, at the mercy of his creditors, and of the gaoler, who wanted his own payment – the 'garnish' to do the minimum for his wretched charges. People visited the prisons and they could gawp in sick fascination at the poor prisoners inside. The Clink, which has been given its name as a general term for prison in English slang, was a short walk from London Bridge, and had existed since it started out as a part of the palace of the Bishop of Winchester, a man whose power would have extended to legal matters as well as religious; the land at Southwark was within the See of Winchester. The place was attacked by the Kentish rebels in 1381 and later it became the main prison for religious offences. Then, after the Great Fire, the city took control and sheriffs were given the power to deal with debtors, hence the use of the place for men like Defoe. It was destined to be burnt to the ground during the Gordon Riots of 1780 and it was never rebuilt.

All Defoe could do to extricate himself was to become the slave of his creditors; he agreed some terms with them and was released, but he still needed help, and luckily that came, in the person of Thomas Neale, who saw in Defoe a kindred spirit, a man who liked risk and enterprise, someone who was happy to try something innovative. The result was involvement in a lottery. Defoe was one of Neale's managers in a scheme which related to profit from ticket sales; his managers received a cut of that profit. Once again, Defoe was up and running, projecting, and taking risks. But he had experienced the highs and the lows of business life in Hanoverian Britain.

Of course he was also a man with an itch to write, and he loved writing polemics, stirring up debate like a good journalist. In 1703 that got him into trouble again, this time with a publication called *The Shortest Way with the Dissenters*. He had foolishly written this with extreme irony, as Swift later did with his writing on the problem of homeless children; in Defoe's case, he wrote in the persona of a Whig expressing extreme views regarding the non-conformists. Defoe himself was brought up a dissenter of course, and he was using irony to show up some prominent aspects of worship which were hypocritical, such as occasional conformity, by which Anglicans in public office could maintain their worship as dissenters. This all stemmed from his aim to show how intractable the established church was in its doctrines, and he underestimated the extent to which his writing would give offence. The Queen herself was moved to act and Defoe was soon a wanted man.

He was on the run for some time, until finally arrested on 21 May 1703 at a house in Spitalfields; two messengers grabbed him and he was interrogated before being taken to Newgate. An informer had been involved receiving £50 for his work. Defoe was in Newgate for almost six months, and we have his own description of the impact of the place, as put into the mouth of his character Moll Flanders, in his novel of the same name:

> I was now fixed indeed; 'tis impossible to describe the terror
> of my mind, when I was first brought in, and when I looked
> around upon all the horrors of that dismal place I looked

upon myself as lost, and that I had nothing to think of, but of going out to the world, and that with the utmost infamy; the Hellish noise, the roaring, swearing and clamour, the stench and nastiness, and all the dreadful crowd of afflicted things that I saw there, joined together to make the place seem an emblem of Hell itself, and a kind of entrance into it.

A few decades later, John Gay was to make Newgate the scene of his ballad opera, *The Beggar's Opera*. The drama attacked the thief-takers and the other figures of the underworld along with the criminal justice system and the corruption, cruelty and hypocrisy therewithin. Daniel Defoe, now a classic author studied across the globe on courses in literature, sat in the squalor of Newgate, like the wretched creations of John Gay.

But before prison, there was something potentially more horrible for him to endure: he was sentenced to the pillory. The pillory could be a very extreme punishment; in 1364 a certain John de Hackford was sent to Newgate for perjury and he was to be pilloried four times, once in each quarter of the city. There was a stone around his neck on which was written, 'false liar.' The whole point about the pillory and the stocks was that they were shaming punishments. A man in the pillory was defenceless, and it was fair game to the scum of the streets to hurl objects at the victim's face. People in that situation were often maimed or blinded, and sometimes even died as a result. Defoe's case was very unusual. He had plenty of friends and so that meant that they were happy to protect him on the day of his disgrace and vulnerability. He was pilloried in Cornhill by the Royal Exchange on 19 July and not far from his own home. But his friends formed a protective barrier and he was saved from harm.

As Paula Backscheider, Defoe's biographer, makes clear, Queen Anne herself was informed of Defoe's condition, and indeed other people were working for his release, including William Penn. Backscheider explains what happened in the attempt to procure a pardon for the writer:

> Nottingham… sent to Newgate for Defoe. The keeper told him that Defoe could not be taken out of London because that

would technically be 'an escape'… Nottingham asked… for a writ of habeas corpus. Defoe's appearance at Windsor on 21 July simply exasperated the Queen. Defoe probably believed he could explain his actions, apologize and simply show that he had talked to private friends…

It didn't work. He stood in the pillory and then served some months in prison. His release came from a powerful voice in the country who had a job for Defoe. This was Godolphin, at that time the Lord Treasurer, who wrote to Harley, a politician with great influence around 1708–14, 'I thank you for the hints about Scotland. Defoe would be the properest [*sic*] person in the world for that transaction.'

What happened was a grander version of the common practice of allowing men to escape jail if they took a place in the army, usually in the line of course. But for Defoe, his potential quality for espionage work was recognised, and that brought about the next phase in his eventful life. Clearly, men in high places had had their eyes on Defoe for some time as a possible agent in the service of the Crown; he was skilled in gathering information, he had excellent communication skills and he knew trade and commerce. He could understand the attitudes, thoughts and conditions of ordinary people and he had a sound grasp of politics.

Defoe's pains and privations in Newgate Prison ended and he became a government agent ready to work in Scotland. Soon, he was to turn his hand to novel-writing which later proved to be another skill within his range. Unlike so many other hapless victims of the criminal justice system of his time, Defoe did not waste away in a dungeon, with his talents and abilities forgotten by the world; his plans and escapades, his financial daring and his will to succeed in a world of movers and shakers of commerce had extricated him from oblivion. The shame of debt he could live with; perhaps such ignominy was so common that many perceived it as bad luck rather than a moral failing. In fact, Defoe was so familiar with the interior of various prisons that it is surprising he didn't include a Newgate narrative in fictional form, as compelling as the tale of Moll or Robinson Crusoe.

2

DR JOHNSON'S DAY IN COURT

Samuel Johnson from his youth had always expressed an interest in the law. He loved to argue on law and generate debates and discussions on legal affairs and theory. His biographer, James Boswell, recalled an anecdote in which the possibility of Johnson's becoming a lawyer was referred to:

> Sir William Scott informs me that, upon the death of Lord Lichfield he said to Johnson, 'What a pity it is, Sir, that you did not follow the profession of the law. You might have been Lord Chancellor...' Johnson, upon this, seemed much agitated, and in an angry tone, exclaimed, 'Why will you vex me by suggesting this, when it is too late?'

Yet he was destined to be a participant in a few notable criminal cases of his time and was to appear at the Old Bailey to support a friend in the dock.

In eighteenth-century Italy, the custom in eating-houses was to provide a fork, but customers had to take their own fruit knives with them when dining out. This fact led to the Italian writer and scholar, Giuseppe Baretti, standing in court at the Old Bailey on 18 October 1769 on a murder charge.

Baretti was born in Turin in 1719 and although he was meant to study law, he always had a passion for literature, and became a talented and widely-read critic. This academic turn of mind served him well when, after drifting across Europe, he came to London looking for a means of subsistence and caught the eye of the administrators of the Royal Academy of Painting. Once employed there as a secretary, it was easy for him to meet literary and artistic people, and soon he was moving in the higher circles of London society, amid talk of aesthetics, art, drama and fine writing. He became acquainted with the Thrale family, brewers and wealthy patrons of the arts and so consequently he met James Boswell and Dr Samuel Johnson.

In 1769 Johnson had been away in Brighton and had also met the Corsican patriot Pasquale Paoli. He was soon to hear what had happened to his friend Baretti. The Italian was walking back to Soho when he was stopped by a prostitute, and as he rebuffed her, she grabbed his testicles and Baretti instinctively turned to strike her. This attack was seen by three roughs who were loitering nearby and they set about him; the woman had screamed and so they assumed Baretti was assaulting her so they pursued him. In defence, at being surrounded by what must have seemed like a gang intent on doing him serious harm, Baretti took out his knife, and in the struggle, the blade entered one of the men who then died of the wounds.

The facts were not clear though. The trial transcripts suggest that witnesses were unsure of the facts and the basic events; a witness, Elizabeth Ward, gave an account that made Baretti seem very aggressive, saying that she was sitting with the girl who accosted him and that he had hit her (Ward) with 'a double fist.' But the barrister questioning her suggested that she had spoken of retaliating by being 'clove down with a patten' – meaning that he should be struck with a wooden over-shoe. She saw Baretti being mobbed by the young men but did not see him draw the knife. This was a crucially important testimony of course.

The court tried to establish whether or not Ward knew the young men who were after Baretti's blood, and she only knew one – he who had kissed her the previous night. This all happened around the Haymarket, a place notorious for gatherings of 'women of the night' and for all kinds of sexual liaisons. Ward followed the gang to see what they might do, and she told the court that after that, she saw the knife drawn, describing the alleged offence in these words, accounting for Baretti's actions:

He ran quite fast, about eight or nine doors up Panton Street, the way where he ran into the house, only the house was farther on;

then I saw his head over their shoulders, turn back. This was when he was gone eight or nine doors up. They all kept close to him. I believe it was then the deceased was stabbed.

The lawyer tried to paint a picture of the woman as being quite a nasty type, drawing her out with regard to her language at the time, and she admitted that she had heard some abuse: 'I remember hearing some say buggerer, or some such name. Some of them called him so.'

One of the men involved called Patman described the confrontation, saying that he had been pushed against Baretti and that he had caught a flash of the blade before Morgan, the man who died, ran in further pursuit. After this, he said:

I never saw Morgan do anything. The gentleman made off half-way up Panton Street. I did not know he had a knife. Morgan ran after him, to take him, and just by the Hole in the Wall, Morgan received a wound. I saw the gentleman strike at him…

Patman had been stabbed and panicked; he felt the blood run down his face; so Morgan ran after a man who by that time was clearly desperately afraid. The self-defence approach to the events was looking likely then. The other man was John Clark, who seems to have held back and let the other two do the most active shoving and grabbing of the Italian. Naturally, both he and Patman claimed that their shoving had been 'light.' But it became clear in the questioning in court that Clark had only a vague idea as to what actually happened and his statements were confused and contradictory. The counsel reminded him that 'the jury are to depend upon something when a man's life is at stake. Have you not declared upon oath that Morgan was the first that said he was stabbed?' Clark's answer contradicted what he had previously told the coroner.

The constable who was called and who took Baretti along to the magistrate at Bow Street, John Fielding, gave a dramatic account of the arrest: 'I immediately sprang to him, seized him by the collar and took the knife and knocked it against a tea-chest to force it in; it was not quite in, and bent the point of it as it is now.' The fruit knives in use then were of a short blade, around three inches, and folded like a pen-knife. Clearly, they had to have a sharp blade to peel an apple, so knives had the potential to do serious harm. The constable ascertained that Baretti was 'a gentleman, and secretary to the Royal Academy and so they went quietly to Bow Street.'

The witness from the hospital where Morgan was treated gave information which seemed to refer to a frenzy rather than a stroke in self-defence, saying that there were three wounds: 'The wound he received in his abdomen was the occasion of his death.' Then the surgeon did some of his own detective work, reporting that Clark was indeed an associate of the women who had been slapped. Clark gave the surgeon two stories and the surgeon made sure that everyone present heard that fact.

In court, Baretti was allowed to give his own account of the facts of that night. Earlier in the day he had gone to a coffee house to see if there was any mail for him, after working on his English-Italian dictionary. He set off back to the club in Soho where the Royal Academicians met, and he described the meeting with the woman:

> There was a woman eight or ten yards from the corner of Panton Street, and she clapped her hands with such violence about my private parts, that it gave me great pain. This I instantly resented, by giving her a blow on the hand.

The woman, seeing he was a foreigner, swore at him, before a man struck him forcefully. There was then a chase, and as Baretti said,

> A great number of people surrounded me presently, many beating me and all damning me on all sides… I could plainly see that my assailants wanted to throw me into a puddle so I cried out murder.

He begged to be taken to Sir John Fielding, and then Sir Joshua Reynolds and other men went to him there, to help and advise. Injuries done to him were observed and noted. He was arrested and detained in Newgate. He could have been tried by people of his own country, but declined, as he told the court: 'I chose to be tried by a jury of this country; for if my honour is not saved, I cannot much wish for the preservation of my life.' Then a key witness told something of what was surely the truth, in complete contrast to the tale told by the three men earlier in court. This was Ann Thomas, who says she saw 'a crowd of people' at the end of a street by the Haymarket, and 'a gentleman run from among them on the side of the way I was… they all ran after him, they were all in a great bustle: I saw but one woman among them…' She made it quite clear that Baretti was running in fear of his life.

When Peter Molini gave an account of Baretti's injuries after that night's violence, the court was in no doubt that Baretti must have acted while in extreme fear, desperate for self-preservation. Molini said,

> As he was complaining of pain in his body, I asked him to strip, that we might see. In looking on his back, I observed a bruise under one shoulder, on the left side, and one a little lower…
> I also saw swelling on his right cheek. Two of the bruises were very visible. His jaw was swelled…

What emerged from other witnesses was a pattern: other men had clearly been accosted in that area in a violent manner. One comment was that the Haymarket was packed with 'abandoned female wretches… generally attended by many men… They will attack you, laying hold of your arm, and are guilty of a very great indecency.' At this point, the true narrative of the lamentable events was unfolding.

All that remained was to present the court with character witnesses, and so Dr Johnson along with other notable men of the time, attended the Old Bailey to have their say. James Boswell, in his famous *Life of Johnson*, explains:

> Never did such a constellation of genius enlighten the awful Sessions House, emphatically called Justice Hall; Mr Burke,

Mr Garrick, Mr Beauclerk and Dr Johnson; and undoubtedly their favourable testimony had due weight with the court and jury.

Boswell adds that Johnson gave his evidence 'in a slow, deliberate and distinct manner, which was uncommonly impressive.' Thanks to the wonder of the internet and the easy availability of the Old Bailey Sessions Papers online, we can read those impressive words today, imagining the 'Great Cham' of literature speaking to the court. After Reynolds and Beauclerk had spoken, Johnson's interchange with the lawyer went as follows:

> **Dr Johnson.** I believe I began to be acquainted with Mr Baretti about the year 53 or 54. I have been intimate with him. He is a man of literature, a very studious man, a man of great diligence. He gets his living by study. I have no reason to think he was ever disordered by liquor in his life. A man that I never knew to be otherwise than peaceable, and a man that I take to be rather timorous.
>
> **Q.** Was he addicted to picking up women in the street?
>
> **Dr Johnson.** I never knew that he was.
>
> **Q.** How is he as to his eye-sight?
>
> **Dr Johnson.** He does not see me now, nor I do not see him. I do not believe he could be capable of assaulting anybody in the street, without great provocation.

Baretti could not have had a better speaker on his behalf: Johnson was always interested in the law and had an extensive knowledge of civil law, as well as a great deal of common sense regarding the practical workings of a trial. The Italian scholar was acquitted of the charges of murder and manslaughter and a verdict of self-defence was returned. But he had tasted the miseries of Newgate and there did exist a nasty side to his character. As Mrs Thrale, wife of his patron, said in a letter in 1784,

> Yesterday received a letter from Mr Baretti, full of the most flagrant and bitter insults concerning my late marriage with Mr Piozzi... he accuses me of murder and fornication in the grossest terms, such as I believe have ever been used, even to his old companions in Newgate.

Yet the friendship of Baretti and Johnson was close and often full of fun, as at one point on a journey to France, the two men had a sprint, which Johnson won. Baretti died on 5 May 1789 and Mrs Thrale wrote that,

> He was a manly character at worst, and died as he had lived, less like a Christian than a philosopher, refusing all spiritual or corporeal assistance... He paid his debts, called in some singular acquaintance, told him he was dying... bid him write his brothers that he was dead, and gently desired a woman who waited to leave him alone.

She was told that Baretti's papers and manuscripts were burnt by his executors. But we do have his books, notably *The Italian Library* of 1747 and *Lettere Famigliari*, a book of travels. His collected works were published in Milan in 1838. He also has the dubious distinction of appearing as a chapter in the classic work of criminal tales, *The Newgate Calendar*, in which the comment on his trial is as follows:

> Those who would consult their own safety should avoid giving offence to others in the street. The casual passenger has, at least, a right to pass unmolested; and he or she that would insult him cannot deserve pity, whatever consequences may follow.

The year before the trial, Johnson had praised Baretti to Boswell, and his words give us no doubt that Johnson's testimony for his friend was genuine and honest. He said of Baretti:

> His account of Italy is a very entertaining book, and sir I know no man who carries his head higher in conversation than Baretti. There are strong powers in his mind. He has not, indeed, many hooks, but with what hooks he had, he grapples firmly.

He had spoken slowly and carefully in court in order to have no doubt or ambiguity in the reception of his words by the jury. Surely, this was a hint relating to Johnson's potential as a man of law, had his career taken a different path.

3

A FREE PARDON FOR SAVAGE

James Boswell, in his great *Life of Johnson*, pauses in his account of the events of 1743 to explain Johnson's friendship with Richard Savage, known mostly to the world at the time as a dangerous character who had killed a man in a tavern brawl in 1727. Savage died in 1743 and Johnson was to write the biography of the man who became a close companion, for Savage was a fellow writer, and the 'Great Cham' of literature (as Oliver Goldsmith called him) felt drawn to his company. Boswell did not approve and wrote that it was difficult to speak impartially of Savage, adding that he was '…marked by profligacy, insolence and ingratitude' and had an 'unregulated mind.'

Yet the fact is that Johnson's biography of his friend is one of the most impressive pieces of writing in that genre of literature; Johnson listened to the younger man, understood his misfortunes and of course received materials with which he could write the book. He expressed a close emotional attachment in this work, in sharp contrast to the other more objective biographies of poets he composed *The Lives of the Poets*. The basis of the friendship is fascinating, as Johnson and Savage were together when both were poor and struggling hacks. Boswell explains that the two men had what we would today call a special bond:

> He told Sir Joshua Reynolds that one night in particular, when Savage and he walked around St James's Square for want of a lodging, they were not at all depressed by their situation, but in high spirits and brimful of patriotism, traversed the square for several hours… and resolved they would stand by their country…

We also know what Savage looked like because Johnson described him: 'He was of middle stature with a thin habit of body, a long visage, coarse features, and melancholy aspect; of a grave and manly deportment...' Regardless of his earlier reputation, in the nineteenth century he was seen as a rake, as Walter Thornbury put it, as 'That clever impostor... who took refuge in the Fleet prison to be safe from his raging creditors...'

Savage knew all about the Grub Street life of the literary hack. In his work *An Author to be Lett* (1729) he wrote the following:

At my first setting out I was hired by a Reverend Prebend to libel Dean Swift for infidelity. Soon after I was employed by Curll to write a merry tale, the wit of which was obscenity. This we agreed to palm upon the world for a posthumous piece for Mr Prior...

He was writing a spoof in this, of the lowest reaches of the world of publishing, and the trade between booksellers (who were also printers) and the hack writers. He knew the world that Johnson had fallen into when he too came to London to find fame with the works of his pen.

There is a special quality in Johnson's life of his friend, and after Savage's death, Johnson wrote to the *Gentleman's Magazine* to explain his unique position as the biographer of the man, writing that he entreated the editor, '...with some degree of assurance... that his life will speedily be published by a person who was favoured with his confidence, and received from himself an account of most transactions which he proposes to mention...'

The public would have known the name of Savage because of the trial for murder he experienced but also for his plays and other works. His tragedy, *Sir Thomas Overbury*, had been produced at Drury Lane in 1723, and he had been involved in the Bangorian Controversy in 1717; this concerned Benjamin Hoadly, the bishop of Bangor, who preached an aggressive sermon against non-jurors, churchmen who had refused to take the Oath of Allegiance to William and Mary of 1688, in which he said that sincerity of belief and private opinions were more important than ecclesiastical power in specific persons in society. Savage enjoyed being involved in such debate of course, and his romps and night-time walks with Johnson and their assertion of patriotism was largely related to that controversy, as the non-jurors were in support of the Stuarts and their Divine Right.

There is no doubt that Savage had a tough life packed with injustice. The facts are easily summarised: he claimed to have been the illegitimate son of the Countess of Macclesfield, after her affair with Lord Rivers; she later married Sir Henry Brett and claimed that the bastard child had died in infancy. Wandering from place to place, he finally settled on a literary career and in London he made friends and managed eventually to have works published; but in 1727, at Robinson's coffee house in the Strand, he was involved in an altercation and was charged with murder and carried off to Newgate to await trial. Fortunately, he had powerful friends and he secured a royal pardon. But he was attracted to trouble and dissension and after moving to Swansea for a while, he travelled back to London, but en route, in Bristol, his wayward and risky lifestyle caught up with him; he was arrested for debt and died in that city in 1743, his funeral expenses being paid for by the gaoler.

Savage's unique position with regard to his life and circumstances gave his poetry an off-beat perspective, and in his poem *The Bastard*, for instance, directly appeals to his mother, making known to all readers what state he was subjected to after her rejection:

Mother, miscalled, farewell – of soul severe,
This sad reflection may yet force one tear:
All I was wretched by to you I owed,
Alone from strangers every comfort flowed...

What happened on that fateful night? According to Johnson, he went from Richmond with two friends, Merchant and Gregory, to London, and there they drank until late; then wandering in the street, they saw a light at Robinson's and went in. There they pushed into a room already occupied, and Johnson relates what happened after that:

> Merchant… petulantly placed himself between the company and the fire, and soon after kicked down a table. This produced a quarrel, swords were drawn on both sides, and one Mr James Sinclair was killed. Savage, having likewise wounded a maid that held him, forced his way with Merchant out of the house… but they were taken in a back-court by one of the company and some soldiers…

Taken to Newgate, he was not placed in a room but in the press yard. This was an area for 'prisoners of note' and for that privilege they had to pay the keeper. There, prisoners could live very much as they would do in their normal lives, and even pay a shilling for the company of a prostitute or for other comforts. In a publication of 1717 called *The History of the Press Yard*, the unknown author wrote that he was there to 'reflect on past indiscretions.' As Johnson noted, Savage was also spared from 'the ignominy of chains.' For eleven shillings a week, in 1717, a prisoner could avoid being fastened by irons and have reasonable comfort.

Two weeks after arrest Savage was in the dock at the Old Bailey before Mr Justice Page, a severe man, who appears fictionalized in Fielding's novel, *Tom Jones*. He was known as a hanging judge and a song was written about him in Dorset with the words, 'God in his rage made old Judge Page.' Johnson dislikes him intensely and in his biased account of the trial he gives the reader Page's voice via Savage, because Savage clearly used to mimic and make fun of the judge long after the trial.

A close look at the trial makes it fairly certain that Savage did not act aggressively or speak threateningly until he drew his sword, and that appears to have been in response to a threat. But the true facts are clouded by Johnson's bias in favour of his friend, of course. He makes it appear that Judge Page controlled and directed the court and jury to such an extent that there was animosity towards this alleged bastard aristocrat:

> The jury then heard the opinion of the judge, that good characters were of no weight against positive evidence, though they might turn the scale where it was doubtful; and that though, when two men attack each other, the death of either is only manslaughter, but where one is the aggressor, as was the case before them, and in pursuance of the first attack, kills the other, the law supposes the action, however sudden, to be malicious...

As Johnson then concluded, Savage had 'No hopes of life.'

Johnson would have us believe that his friend was about to die because of the words of 'a bawd, a strumpet and his mother' until a saviour came in the person of the Countess of Hertford. But actually, as research has shown, Lord Tyrconnel was the real rescuer. Tyrconnel was John Brownlow, who became the fifth baronet, and also took the title of Baron Charleville in the Irish peerage. He was brought up by Lady Mason, his grandmother, and she had also worked hard on behalf of Savage, so they knew each other through that connection.

Whoever related the sad tale of Savage's life of rejection and hatred at the hands of his true mother, it saved his neck. But the life of dissolution continued, and Savage was destined to end his life behind bars. Tyrconnel did his best for some time, arranging financial support. But there was eventually a rift between them, as so often happened with Savage and his acquaintances. Johnson explains: 'Lord Tryconnel was accused by Mr Savage of some actions which scarcely any provocations will be thought sufficient to justify, such as seizing what he had in his lodgings, and other instances of wanton cruelty...' But this is hardly the behaviour of the man who, in 1730, recommended Savage for the post of Poet Laureate and who was generous and kindly towards Savage to a great extent. He was to outlive Savage, dying in 1754.

Savage was in debt and the creditors pursued him. His best move appeared to be to return to London; he had left there four years before, and now, in 1743, he found himself taken prisoner yet again and confined in the Bristol Newgate. 'Newgate' had become a generic term for a city prison – such an institution existed also, for example, in Green Street, Dublin. Thirty years after Savage's stay, the great reformer John Howard visited the Bristol gaol where Savage spent his last months and was impressed: 'I found it clean, considering it was so crowded and so close. It was scraped and whitewashed once a year before the Act preserving the health of prisoners' and he noted that there were fifteen rooms for debtors. In fact, of all the records of prisoners we have through the eighteenth century, that of Richard Savage in Bristol is surely the most surprisingly humane and atypical. The reason for that is in the acts of one man: Abel Dagge.

Johnson wrote that,

> He was treated by Mr Dagge, the keeper of the prison, with great humanity; was supported by him at his own table without any certainty of recompense; had a room to himself to which he could at any time retire without disturbance.

This was remarkably liberal and kind for that time and place; Dagge was indeed a rare individual. He had been deeply affected by John Wesley's preaching, and one commentator notes that 'So effective was Mr Wesley's preaching at the Bristol Newgate that Mr Dagge, the keeper, was much affected at the lives of the people on whom the power of God came.' A year after this conversion in 1740, the aldermen ordered that Wesley should not be admitted again into the gaol.

Luck was on his side. Not very long before this, in 1683, a keeper called Isaac Dennis had reportedly been cruel to his charges, as a book published at the time states. One instance of this abuse was this:

> ...he took me by the arm and threw me to the door, and was going to throw me downstairs; I then being cutting of corks,

---

had a cork-knife in my hand, and he let me lay down the knife… Then threw it at me, and broke the shin of my leg very badly…

In contrast, Savage's ill-fated life was suddenly sunny as he met this reformed and kind gaoler.

Savage's later biographer describes the prison life in Bristol in more detail than Johnson, including the fact that 'Savage's favourite recreation at this time was to stand at the open door of the prison and watch the passers-by, while he breathed the sweetness of the June air…' and that there, 'he experienced a sense of freedom which neither wealth nor fame could have imparted.'

Dagge also did the almost unthinkable: he went for country walks with Savage and they stopped at taverns for beer and conversation; admittedly, his charge was a debtor, not a hardened criminal, but even so, that was a most liberal and staggeringly atypical treatment of a prisoner at the time. Savage's Edwardian biographer paints an idyllic picture of the country walks: 'So, as they walked, Savage plucked Dagge's sleeve, put finger to lip and pointed at the swaying stem on which a linnet perched; stopped him to hear the murmur of distant water, or to breathe in the sweetness of new-mown hay.' This seems to be pushing the truth somewhat but there is no doubt that the gaoler was receptive to the oddity and buoyant spirit of his charge.

Savage managed to carry on writing while behind bars and this led to yet one more mistake in a life packed with a catalogue of errors. He wrote a poem called *London and Bristol Delineated*. As John expressed it,

…whatever insults he might have received during the latter part of his stay at Bristol, once caressed, esteemed and presented with a liberal collection, he could forget on a sudden his danger… and publish a satire by which he might reasonably expect that he should alienate those who had supported him…

Some lines from the poem show what the attitude he took was, and how self-destructive it seems:

> In a dark bottom sunk, O Bristol now,
> With native malice, lift thy lowering brow!
> What friendship can'st thou boast? What honours claim?
> To thee each stranger owes and injured name.

On 31 July 1743 he died in his cell. He had earlier waved a hand at Dagge and said he had something to say to him but then said he had forgotten what it was. That was their last meeting. An anonymous artist drew the building at the Bristol Newgate where his room could be seen, adding, 'This is a view of the keeper's compartment. Savage died in a second-storey room.' The scene shows an ordinary street, with a water pump, and behind, slabs of stone and rows of plain windows with mesh over the glass – the only hint that this might be a prison.

Of all Samuel Johnson's criminal associates (and he had more than a few, as we have seen) Richard Savage has to be the one friend who provided Johnson with what can be called not only a great literary biography but an early work of the genre of true crime – at least in some respects. After all, it contains a biased account of an Old Bailey trial, accounts of prison life and indeed the writer's own acquaintance with a notorious rake and drifter whose soul burned with injustice and a sense of alienation. Johnson, a man whose emotions were often worn on his sleeve and who had an immense capacity for love and charity, found his understanding of human transgressions tested to the full, and the result was one of his finest literary works.

Looking back on the life of Savage, and his time in both prisons, the London and Bristol Newgates, it is hard to resist the conclusion that he represents a recurrent figure in literature. He exemplifies the drifting, feckless poet of the streets, the balladeer, part with the motley of the jester and part having the solemn countenance of the satirist who feels bitterness at every turn in his journey through life. He eventually found friends and patrons, even receiving a pension at one time; yet there was a sick resentment in him and perhaps a sad self-hatred. On the surface, it looks as though his work was fuelled by nothing more than easy scorn, but there was a talent in him which Johnson saw.

Nothing that happened to him failed to provide 'material' and even his part in the murder, and some lines from *The Bastard* present a muddled yet impassioned reference to the effects of that experience:

Is chance a guilt? That my disastrous heart
For mischief never meant must ever smart?
Can self-defence be sin? Ah plead no more!
What though no purposed malice stained thee o'er?

A strong theme in his poetry, compelling and insistent, but not well expressed at times, is this self-searching, a confusion of emotional narrative, sometimes self-pitying and at times stringent and incisive, explaining his own unhappy spirit to himself and to the reader. Prison life, in the later stage, at least brought some kind of purposeful reflection and philosophical comfort. But the rage never really left.

4

THE MACARONI PARSON

Even some of the highest churchmen and politicians in the land can have prison as their fate, and such was the case with Dr Dodd. In an age of patronage, nepotism and corruption, it was always likely for a man of status to transgress, and Dodd had certainly yielded to temptation.

One of the oldest words for 'prison' is *compter*, a word possibly coming from the idea of 'account,' and therefore paying one's account with society. In London there were several and the Wood Street Compter, which does now not exist except as part of a cellar, was one of the most feared in the city, being opened in 1555. An early commentator wrote that the place was for 'the miserable multitude of distressed prisoners' and that in the early seventeenth century there were 'in number fifty poor men or thereabouts, lying upon bare boards, still languishing in great need.'

It was destroyed in the Great Fire of 1666 and then rebuilt, and in its second incarnation one of its distinguished residents was a learned doctor of divinity, a man who had been chaplain to the King: The Rev. Dr William Dodd, forger. At that time the new compter was on the street and not set back, allowing prisoners to reach out a hand and beg from passing citizens. Dodd found himself in a tough and grim place. His offence was to forge a bond in the name of his one-time patron, Lord Chesterfield; this was for a huge amount for the time, that of £4,200. Forgery was a serious capital offence and therefore the risk was massive.

Dodd was the son of the Vicar of Bourne in Lincolnshire, and had excelled as a scholar, starting out as a poor sizar, a scholar receiving funds from the college for his study who had to wait on the more wealthy scholars as a servant. In spite of this lowly position, Dodd did very well at Clare Hall, Cambridge, where he impressed in his studies. He also earned income from his writing and from public speaking, being a first-class communicator and also a man of fashion and wit. He graduated in 1749 and went to London, spending two years living by his pen, as so many had done before him. Then strangely, he married someone who brought no wealth: Mary Perkins, in the language of the time, 'of no family.'

From that point, he became a man who lived beyond his means, obviously with high ambitions and plenty of talent for sale. Yet, as with so many in his age, his extravagance led to debtors' prison, and he was only rescued from that when friends told his father. This situation was the germ of his future career because the church was the natural social move to try to establish himself back in society. He was ordained in Cambridge by the Bishop of Ely and took a curacy at West Ham.

His writing helped to make a name in the right kind of society, particularly when he published his book on Shakespeare, *The Beauties of Shakespeare*, and mixed in literary circles as well as in religious ones, as his sermons were also successful; this was a time in which volumes of sermons sold well. It was the era of the rise of Methodism and there was a readership for religious writings. He was made a lecturer at St James, Garlick Hill in London and then at St Olave's where Pepys had worshipped. Still his reputation grew and he also had the position of chaplain at a new refuge for fallen women at Magdalen House. Dodd was a rare spirit, indulging in both selfish attempts at preferment in an age of nepotism and 'jobs for the boys' but also in charitable works, founding a society for the relief of poor debtors, for instance, and he was also part of the initiative which established what later became the Royal Humane Society.

Yet he always possessed an unstable personality with an addiction to risk. The society he lived in was one of notable extremes of rich and poor, and when a man fell, his descent was to the lower depths of Hell, even though he had known the heights of power and influence. Dodd knew the right moves to take in order to at least try to stay solvent and successful, but there was always a chance that he would overreach himself. For example, he had extra income from tutoring and housing boys of good backgrounds at his West Ham home and fortune was on his side at first, because he was noted by George III, who made him chaplain-in-ordinary, one of 36 such who work in a rotation at St James's. However, as social preferment often works by recommendation, his name was dropped to the Earl of Chesterfield as a potential tutor for his son, Philip Stanhope. That was the foreboding of his future disgrace, and yet paradoxically at this time he also gained his doctorate – a doctor of laws from Cambridge.

Then, in the late 1760s, he transformed his lifestyle from that of a preacher and tutor who wrote as a hobby, into 'a life of ostentation and luxury' as Lord Birkenhead puts it in his account of Dodd's life. At that time, he won a lottery prize of £1,000 pounds, and that probably encouraged his tendency towards risk and speculation; he should have progressed well, because he also had two benefices, in an age of clerical pluralism, when a man could have these ecclesiastical incomes for doing no or very little parish work. He made a house at Ealing his main abode, and kept his young men for tutoring work when he could spare the time. He even bought a share of the Charlotte Street Chapel in Bloomsbury, from which a later incumbent, according to a writer in *Notes and Queries* in 1896, made 'a thousand pounds a year in pew rents.'

The ominous event of 1773 then happened: his employer, Philip, became Earl of Chesterfield – the man he was destined to attempt to swindle. But before that he indulged in some other activities which made him enemies and increased his negative image around town. One of these was his publication of a novel called *The Sisters*, in which there are elements which would scandalise the more conventionally moral in the higher circles of society.

This was followed by a scandal of a much higher level, such that it made Dodd leave London for the country for several months. What happened was that a vacancy arose: a very lucrative living in London became available, and the Lord Chancellor had the power to place the new man in the position. This was Lord Apsley, so Dodd did what many in the eighteenth century did – he approached Lady Apsley with the offer of £3,000 if she could arrange for him to be the chosen man. Lady Apsley showed this to her husband, and then the King was told. The result was that Dodd lost his royal chaplaincy; it was the beginning of the end for him, because the attempt at bribery went public. There was even a satirical drama on stage depicting the affair; the papers went to town attacking him. He was corrupt and had been found out – the worst sin in an age of corruption and bribery. Dodd had been a very busy writer in the ten years before this faux pas, writing all kinds of material, and some of this had been to win favour, such as the *Ode to the Marchioness of Granby* (1759) and *An Epistle to a Lady Concerning Truths in Religion* (1753). The Georgian years worked by the sale of offices and sinecures were common; there was even a printed guide called *The Red Book* which listed the sinecures and their emoluments. Maybe Dodd thought he was doing something totally normal but he was wrong. He had stepped too far over the line, being too extreme even for a society that functioned on a 'jobs for the boys' system.

He gave a last sumptuous dinner for special guests and a farewell sermon before retreating into rural banishment. When he returned he was ruined. In desperation, this man of chance and risk made his fatal move into criminality. He approached a broker called Robertson, with the intention of using his association with Chesterfield to gain a huge profit on a bond. He told Robertson that he was raising a sum for the coming of age of 'a nobleman.' Robertson's task was to find a person or firm who would give a loan based on the bond and eventually he found Fletcher and Peach, who gave the £4,200 of the bond with the forged signature. Robertson earned £100 for the negotiation.

But it appears that the firm noticed a blot or mark on the bond and they became suspicious. When they showed this to Chesterfield to check, he was sure that it was forged. Robertson and Dodd were traced and arrested. All varieties of forgery, uttering and counterfeiting were dealt with severely and they were considered capital felonies; in the monumental legal work of Blackstone, he wrote that 'There is now hardly a case possible to be conceived wherein forgery, that tends to defraud, whether in the name of a real or fictitious person, is not made a capital crime.' It was extremely unusual for penalties of pillory, fines or imprisonment to replace death by hanging. At this point, Dodd was taken to the Wood Street Compter to await trial at the Old Bailey.

The trial took place on 19 February 1777, and began with a long and involved debate on the legal problem of Robertson being called as a witness, and his competency to act as such before the Grand Jury, when they had to decide whether or not there was a bill to accept and an indictment of Dodd to be accepted. Basically, Robertson was doing what has been done since time immemorial: speaking up so as to have lenient treatment. The matter of his admissibility was not fully resolved, however, and the decision was deferred, later to be put before the judges at Serjeants' Inn for a decision; when Dodd pleaded guilty and the trial proceeded, he must have thought that he had a chance of saving his neck, mainly because of Robertson's position as a supposed dupe of Dodd himself, an innocent who did not realise the implications of the document. After all, the forged bill was conceived and executed by Dodd. Here was a notable clergyman, a doctor of law and a former King's Chaplain, standing in the dock, a common felon in general opinion, and likely to end his life dancing on the end of a rope at Tyburn.

Eventually, there was an indictment containing the following important words:

> [he] feloniously did falsely make forge and counterfeit, and cause to procure to be falsely made… and willingly act and assist in false making… a certain paper, partly written and partly printed, purporting to be a bond, and to be signed by the Right Honourable the Earl of Chesterfield and to be sealed and delivered by the said Earl…

Robertson naturally covered himself. This was the crucial part of his examination:

Q.	Look at the letter. Is it the same letter?
Robertson.	It is.
Q.	Did you receive the same letter from Dr Dodd?
Robertson.	Yes, at his own lodgings at Argyll Buildings.
Q.	Was the name of Dodd written on it before you came, or in your presence?
Robertson.	He wrote William Dodd on it upon the bond in my presence.

Dodd was, of course, a skilled public speaker; when his time came to speak in his own defence he made the most of it, saying: 'My Lords, I have creditors, honest men, who will lose much by my death; I hope for the sake of justice towards them some mercy will be shown to me.' His speech exhibits all the skill and cunning one would expect from a powerful orator and he even tried the emotional pull of his wife's situation: 'I have a wife, my Lords, who for 27 years has lived an unparalleled example of conjugal attachment and felicity, and whose behaviour during this crying scene would draw tears of approbation, I am sure, from the most inhuman.' It didn't work: the jury found him guilty, but did at least request Dodd to the mercy of the King.

He was taken back to Newgate to await his fate; there he wrote a book entitled *Thoughts in Prison* which was later published. When he returned to court for sentencing, the appeal to mercy had been denied; Johnson's plea was read out, but Dodd had concentrated his mind on the gallows. Johnson did not accept defeat on the matter, though; he wrote to the Lord Chancellor and to the Lord Chief Justice. Eighteen years previously, he had written, in an *Idler* essay about prisons, that 'the misery of gaols is not half their evil; they are filled with every corruption which poverty and wickedness can generate between them.' Dodd had already experienced that, while waiting for his trial; then there was the question of hanging. We know from Boswell that Dodd wrote several times, from gaol, to Johnson, and in one of these he expresses his wish to escape the noose and to 'pass the remainder of my days in penitence and prayer. I would bless his [the King's] clemency and be humbled.'

There was a petition, signed by 23,000 people, asking for the pardon of Dodd, but to no avail. Popular feeling did sway in Dodd's favour, as Lord Birkenhead wrote, 'The promise made and broken, and the fact that Lord Chesterfield had given evidence – though he could not refuse – caused men to think that the prisoner had been ill-used.'

Once again, Dr Johnson had something to say. He wrote a sermon headed 'The Convict's Address to His Unhappy Brethren' and when Dodd had been hanged and the affair was all concluded, he said, 'Sir, as Dodd got it from me to pass as his own, while that could not do him any good, there was an implied promise that I should not own it.' Johnson also, with reference to Dodd's situation and the writing of the farewell sermon, made his famous remark that 'When a man knows he is to be hanged in a fortnight, it concentrates the mind wonderfully.'

Then time was up: he was taken to Tyburn and hanged. His devoted wife lived on for ten years, as Birkenhead wrote, 'insane and poor.' *The Newgate Calendar* has the most vivid account of his last moments, as he died alongside another man called Joseph Harris:

> It is impossible to give an idea of the immense crowds that thronged the streets from Newgate to Tyburn. When the prisoners arrived at the fatal tree, and were placed in the cart, Dr Dodd exhorted his fellow-sufferer in so generous a manner as to testify he had not forgot the duty of a clergyman… Just before the parties were turned off, Dr Dodd whispered to the executioner. What he said cannot be known; but it was observed that the man had no sooner driven the cart away than he ran immediately under the gibbet and took hold of the Doctor's legs, as if to steady the body, and the unhappy man appeared to die without pain.

One of the most repulsive characters of the time was George Selwyn, a man who had a morbid fascination with the scaffold; Anthony Storer wrote to Selwyn, knowing he would relish an account of Dodd's last minutes. He describes a farcical scene:

> The executioner took both the hat and the wig off at the same time. Why he put on his wig again I do not know, but he did and the doctor took off his wig a second time, and then tried on a nightcap which did not fit him… He put on his nightcap and he certainly had a smile on his countenance…

Dodd was said by some to look 'stupid with despair' and that on the journey, many saw his corpse-like face framed in the coach window.

According to one tradition, friends took the body to the great surgeon, John Hunter, who was to try to restore life. But as one Victorian writer noted, 'Owing to the bigness of the crowd, precious minutes and even hours, were lost before the body arrived, and by this time all hope of revivication was gone.' Dodd was hanged along with a teenager who had robbed a man of just less than thirty shillings; this man, Harris, was quickly dispatched.

The whole story was moralized as a tale against extravagance: Dodd was very much a man of his time, but he overreached himself and offended one of the most influential men in the land. As to his writings, he produced dozens of books and tracts along with many sermons. Yet surely he would not be remembered had it not been for Dr Johnson and for the massive popularity of the *Newgate Calendar*.

The myths and hearsay went on. In 1807, Robert Southey, writing as a pretend visitor to England, wrote this of the case:

> It was long believed that his life had been preserved by connivance of the executioner; that a waxen figure had been buried in his stead, and that he had been conveyed over to the continent.

5

ANOTHER WRITER IN NEWGATE

William Cobbett, remembered mostly perhaps as the author of the classic *Rural Rides* (1830), was always likely to spend time behind bars, given his argumentative temperament and his habit of annoying those who abused power. Cobbett, a farmer as well as a writer and provocative journalist, started his periodical, the *Political Register*, in 1802, and soon found himself at the centre of a group of radical thinkers. Long before the advent of Chartism, there were people from all quarters who wanted political change, specifically in the franchise, and this was to become something that Cobbett espoused.

He served in the army and found widespread corruption there; his writings took him into trouble and he ran away to America, where again he could not resist being embroiled in controversy and publishing. Back in England, he started his family farm but saw such much abuse and inhumanity around him that his pen remained active in the causes he valued. Yet, the episode that led to his spell in Newgate was related not to the vote for working men or secret ballots, but to the use of flogging in the army.

The lash was used in prisons and in the armed services and it was applied mercilessly and sometimes with the knowledge that the victim would die. This barbarity had become an accepted part of the military as well as the prison regimes across the land.

Until the mid-nineteenth century, offenders were whipped, but there was no strict regulation on usage and the number of lashes; women were whipped until 1820 and public flogging was practised until the 1830s. In previous centuries, one of the duties of the town hangman was to whip offenders 'at the cart's tail.' Even outside of prison, as a direct corporal punishment, it was used, but with several moral difficulties attached, as this report from the *Inverness Journal* for 1817 shows, after a woman called Grant had been flogged through the streets of the town for 'intoxication and bad behaviour' and reporters had noted 'public and repeated flagellation on the naked body of a woman is revolting to our general ideas of decency and humanity...' They also stated:

> We doubt whether such an exhibition is calculated to amend our morals: on the unfortunate object in question, (a young and handsome woman) the hardened and indifferent audacity with which she bore and ridiculed the punishment, showed that it failed of that effect – so much indeed, notwithstanding this third flagellation, we understand that she returned from her banishment the same evening...

When used by the prison authorities and the military, there were no such qualms or moral dilemmas. The cat o' nine tails was the instrument of pain used. Although in the 1860s its use was restricted and the birch was to be used on juveniles.

In prison, the cat o' nine tails, a multi-tailed whip made of knotted thongs around two and a half feet long, designed to lacerate the skin, was used. The nine tails are the ends of the plaited ropes. These are made by weaving together three ropes. Prisons had a flogging frame that was used for flogging; the frame was a huge x-shape of wood with a thick pad across the centre and foot-straps down at the lowest level. There were straps also for the prisoner's wrists and their body would be held upright by two straps from the very top of the frame.

In the army, flogging was administered in inhumane and cruel ways; the trigger for Cobbett's offensive essay was an incident at Ely which was reported as a mutiny. In fact a group of half-starved soldiers complained to their officers of a withdrawal of provision ('a stoppage of the knapsacks') and their aggression was rewarded by a sentence of five hundred lashes to be given to the ringleaders followed by a courts martial. Cobbett, in his soldiering days, had witnessed such barbarity, and he wrote about this, explaining that he had been 'Unable to endure the sight, and to hear the cries without swooning away.' He added that he and others would do their best to help: 'We used to lift them back a little way, take off their stocks and unbutton their shirt collars, and they came to after a little while…'

Flogging in the army could be the most cruel and brutal of all, across the spectrum of punishments in a barbaric time. In 1831 three men were flogged in the armoury yard at Birdcage Walk. The sight was so dreadful that a meeting was called to raise a petition against such practice. But later in 1836 it was still widely reported, as in an account in the *Companion to the Times* in which flogging was restricted to cases of mutiny, insubordination and violence, but was still a very extreme punishment.

After the flogging at Ely, Cobbett could not contain his fury and disgust. He wrote that he did not know what sort of place Ely was but, 'I should like to know how the inhabitants looked one another in the face while this scene was exhibiting in their town.' His biographers agree that after the long outburst in the *Register*, a writ was coming his way. The authorities had him as a marked man. Naturally, he worried about the consequences for his family of an arrest and a guilty verdict. It would be a felony, and so he would forfeit land and possessions if found guilty. It was in the early part of 1810 when he was concerned that the Attorney General had him in his sights. Then, fate stepped in with a furore on a larger scale, concerning yet another injustice: there was an expedition to Walcheren. This had been in the previous year, when a landing in Holland by the army failed miserably. It had been an expedition aiming to capture Walcheren, the island where Flushing stands. A fleet carrying 40,000 men took part, and everything went wrong, including arguments in the high command and dysentery among the troops; after a huge death toll, the whole business was suspended and an ignominious return home followed. One commander was attacked in print by a certain Gale Jones, and the latter was dragged to Newgate. Sir Francis Burdett wrote in the *Register*, on the injustice of the Jones case, and after a mob in the streets and public disorder, Burdett was taken to the Tower. Cobbett could not resist writing a response in which he bewailed the injustice:

> To bereave a man of life, or by violence to confiscate his estate, without accusation or trial, would be so gross and notorious an act of despotism as must at once convey the alarm of tyranny throughout the whole kingdom.

The writ of *habeas corpus* had been suspended so that a person could be in gaol without trial.

Cobbett was guilty of a criminal libel. A substantial part of the material relating to his defence was, alarmingly, inadmissible in court. The trail was therefore loaded against him from the start and everything depended on the jury. He was guilty but had to wait for sentencing; then on 5 July after spending four days in the King's Bench Prison, he was given two years, and the judge's summing up included these words: 'The present libel goes to subvert society itself... The army, against whom this libel was directed, called on the court for justice against its traducer...'

He was not only in prison but he also had to pay the immense sum of £1,000 to the King on release. He was allotted a top floor room in the gaoler's quarters, and to make matters worse, his wife was pregnant at the time and she soon after gave birth to a daughter who died only three weeks old.

Cobbett had no choice but to run his farm from a distance via his sons; he also managed to keep the *Register* alive, as Leigh Hunt was to do for his *Examiner* journal a little later. He was never a man to waste any time and behind bars he studied economics and planned a book on the subject. He was in prison at a time when England experienced one of its most sustained periods of deep and violent social unrest: the rise of the Luddite machine-wrecking. The government, at war with Napoleon, was coping with trouble on the domestic front also, and that was daily escalating. There was even the unthinkable: Prime Minister Spencer Perceval was assassinated by John Bellingham, yet another ex-prisoner with a grudge.

Cobbett must have been sorely frustrated at not being outside, active in the fight for liberty and justice. He had to be quarrelling with someone, and as his biographers point out, he was siding more and more with the ordinary people and seeing the appalling abuse of power by the wealthy and corrupt more clearly than ever before. Sir Francis Burdett's offending essay had in its title, 'Remarks to His Constituents on the Power of Imprisonment by the House of Commons…' It explained the mind-set of all those like Cobbett who were furious at the cruelties and whimsical abuse of principles and morals, exercised largely through a paranoia that what had happened in France might happen here.

Cobbett could never resist criticism and questioning of policies and legal wrongs wherever he found them. Even in his most famous work, the *Rural Rides*, he writes about Hampshire and pauses to analyse the assizes and the law with regard to poaching. Referring to the hanging of two men at Winchester, he adds, 'I know very well that there is a law for this, but what I shall endeavour to show is that the law ought to be altered.' There is so much of the man in that last sentence. He liked nothing better than to have a cause and to highlight the exercise of power by those who delighted in seeing others suffer. Five years after his release, he was in America again, in many ways a changed man, interested in wider matters than party faction and corruption. Remedies for such abuses as he saw also lay in education and in the principle that knowledge is power, and that ordinary people could, through education, win the fight in a different location than in the streets thirsting for blood and vengeance.

What was Newgate like around 1820? For the poor prisoners and the habitual criminals, it was mostly a regime of repression and solitary confinement. We have several accounts of visits there and one of the most detailed is from an anonymous writer who produced a work in 1818 called *Old Bailey Experience*. In that work he writes at length on the treatment of prisoners and he makes a special point about the use of solitary confinement:

But if a mind, totally void of sources of reflection, be shut up in a cell for years, or even for months, what can be expected but that every day will stultify its powers and at last render it callous and unimpressionable…

At the time of this writer, the penal laws were such that the prisons were crammed with all kinds of offenders, and he lists the most common crimes, including the slang names for them, as in the example of pickpockets known as buzzmen, or coiners known as bit-makers.

Newgate was a place where the underclasses were dumped out of sight, but it was also for 'gentlemen' like Cobbett, and for him it was very different. Consideration was always given to anyone with status as we have seen in the case of Richard Savage.

As with so many in the late Georgian years who had dared to speak out against a repressive regime with government spies, repressive legal measures, military might against the poor and a cruel criminal law, Cobbett had paid a heavy price for caring and crying out for justice. His was such a high talent that he never could be silenced. Prison for him was nowhere near as comfortable as it was for Leigh Hunt or William Combe, although he was allowed some home comforts, but it confirmed his profound hatred and contempt for the wrongful use of power. The experience resonated throughout his career and in his 1830 masterpiece, *Rural Rides*, he reflects at one point on what he achieved in campaigning for the economic well-being of farm labourers, writing:

> …when I reflect that there must necessarily be, now some hundreds of families and shortly many thousands of families, in England who are and will be, through my means, living well instead of being half-starved, I cannot but feel myself consoled; I cannot but feel that I have some compensation for the sentence passed on me by Lord Ellenborough, Grose, Leblanc and Bayley.

He had all the names of those who presided on his case imprinted on his memory. Yet in complete contrast, at about the same time that he was feeling good about such success, Charles Greville, the diarist and clerk to the Privy Council, wrote: 'Cobbett… writes to inflame the minds of the people who are already set in motion and excited by all the events which have happened abroad…' On other occasions Greville referred to Cobbett as a 'bad character' and a 'blackguard' – and so we have a clear image of how he was seen, as the writer who arguably most incensed the authorities in one of the most turbulent decades of English history. As he contemplated with satisfaction upon personal victories, his reputation as a firebrand spread widely across the upper ranks of society, a fact which troubled him very little indeed.

6

JANE AUSTEN'S AUNT BEHIND BARS

British gaols at the turn of the eighteenth century were places of terror and oblivion; everyone had a horrendously miserable time inside these places and many died of gaol fever. The minds which created these places specialized in the art of spawning misery and despair. It is hard today to envisage the sheer depth of desolation the Georgian prison contained. Most inmates were either debtors or common criminals but a few were wealthy, middle-class folk who had strayed across the line into illegality. One of these was a Mrs Jane Leigh-Perrot, and she was Jane Austen's aunt.

Before her story is told, we need to move forward in time a little to understand something of the gaol she was destined to inhabit: Ilchester. We have this insight because just a few years after Mrs Leigh-Perrot was behind bars there was a scandal at her prison.

This imprisonment and treatment of radical leaders in the early years of the nineteenth century came to national attention with the case of Henry Hunt, the man who had spoken at the Peterloo Massacre. The focus of attention was Ilchester Gaol where Hunt was sent after sentencing. Hunt, known as 'Orator' after his rousing speeches given in London in 1816–17, was born in Wiltshire, and became a radical thinker, believing in what he termed 'mass pressure' – a non-violent concept simply involving a radical line of thought in the minds of the majority – the workers, who had no vote and who were subject to the vagaries of economics and to the severity of the law. He became MP for Blackburn and while he was in gaol writing his memoirs, this town compiled a petition: 500 people complained of the harsh treatment Hunt was subject to in Ilchester. Hunt himself petitioned to parliament as well, such was his miserable state. But he was also revolted by the treatment of other prisoners at the gaol. In March 1822 in parliament, John Hobhouse told the House about the prison:

> He called upon the House to look at the total absence of control in the prison. The gaoler was not checked by the surgeon, the surgeon by the coroner, nor the coroner by the magistrates. Let them remember the abuses and cruelties proved: Hillier loaded with irons and beheld, so loaded, without interference from the magistrates, and Mary Cuer, with her new-born child, exposed to cold and hunger. Let members advert to the badness of the bread, and the impurity of the water – to the absence of air and sunshine, and to the presence of instruments of torture unparalleled but by those brought over in the Spanish Armada…

There had been an enquiry and the interviews with staff had highlighted these abuses. William Bridle, the turnkey, was tried for his cruelties. An old man called Charles Hill, for instance, had been confined there for fifteen years. He reported that prisoners were locked up from 5 p.m. to 7 a.m. The gaol was built near a river and parts of it were below water level; the gaol was flooded to a depth of fourteen inches and gaol fever often raged there. Sometimes, prisoners due to appear in court were not taken there for fear of their fever infecting the assembly at the court. Gaol fever was a powerful influence on the running of the courts at the time. At times, bacteria played a more dominant part in the criminal justice system than the legal profession itself.

Mr Alderman Wood told the House, responding to a petition by another prisoner:

> As to the gaoler's own house, there were proofs to show that it was kept open to unseasonable hours, and sometimes all night, while it was a scene of riot, drunkenness and gambling… it was customary for people to gather there to gamble… a clergyman of the neighbourhood had lost 18 guineas there one night…

One of the worst atrocities was the case of a man called Gardner, who had been put in solitary confinement, into a 'dark dungeon' then chained to his bed, his head shaved and a 'blister' applied to his scalp by the hand of another prisoner. This must have been a plaster of some kind. The man tried to rub it off by scraping his head on the wall. That made the turnkey apply a straitjacket to the unfortunate man.

These abuses were caused by the new staff, people succeeding a number of earlier gaolers who appear to have run the gaol fairly well and sent a large sum of money to the gaoler's family. Ilchester was not a den of iniquity in 1807 when Dr Lettsom inspected the place for the *Gentleman's Magazine*. He reported that the rooms were furnished with a bedstead and straw and that the inmates were washed and the men shaved regularly in the cold or warm baths near the main gate.

By 1819, when Hunt was there, things had changed, and William Bridle was the man responsible. At Wells assizes in August 1822, he appeared in court, charged with 'intent to injure' Mary Cuer and James Hillier. The prosecution was brought for the Crown by the Attorney General. In the case of Hillier, the gaoler had applied the blister – a hot poultice probably – after shutting Hillier in a dark cell, and later fitting a straitjacket. He had shut Mary Cuer, with her new baby, in the dark cell from the 10–23 November, providing only bread and water. When she was given water, she had to drink it from a bucket. Not surprisingly, in the winter with those deprivations, both mother and child became seriously ill and barely survived the ordeal.

The magistrates were cleared of any failings and surprisingly, although Bridle had been sacked in July 1821, they said good things about him. Sir John Acland said that Bridle was 'an honest and meritorious officer.' Yet strangely, a certain Elizabeth Smith who was to testify in support of Mary did not turn up at court. The jury found Bridle guilty only in the case of Hillier and a sentence was passed a week later: Bridle was fined £50 and he was to be kept at the Marshalsea until he could pay the sum.

Henry Hunt was released in 1823 and had a party in London. He later published an account of the prison in his book, *A Peep into a Prison, or the Inside of Ilchester Bastille.*

All this, a chronicle of terrible suffering and abuse, happened just two decades after the lady who introduced Jane Austen to Bath's cultural delights was a guest of His Majesty George III in the same gaol.

It all began with the simplest of everyday pleasures – shopping. People with plenty of cash to spare naturally cultivate the art of relishing the pleasures of what we call 'retail therapy' and that recreation was as strong in Austen's time as it is now. In 1799 Jane Austen's aunt, Mrs Leigh-Perrot, called in at a linen-draper's shop in Bath to buy some white lace. When her purchase had been packed, there were whispers among the staff, and the manager asked her to open the package. Inside, there was a card of black lace as well as the white lace she had bought. Was it a mistake by the assistant, as Jane insisted?

The Leigh-Perrots were very well off and the woman certainly did not need to steal anything. Aunt Jane's husband, James Leigh, was born in Harpenden in 1735, and later added Perrot to his name after being the fortunate beneficiary of his great-uncle Thomas. He married Jane Cholmeley in 1764. By the time of the alleged shoplifting he was a wealthy and influential man. We have a description of him by Jane Austen's nephew:

He was a man of considerable power, with much of the wit of his uncle, the Master of Balliol, and wrote very clever epigrams and riddles, some of which, though without his name, found their way into print.

The Leigh-Perrots took a house in Bath after James had developed the very painful condition of gout; it was thought that taking the Bath waters would improve his health and so they took a house at Number 1, Paragon Buildings, where Jane Austen stayed with them on a few occasions.

Shop-lifting of items such as cloth was very common then. Daniel Defoe makes the theft of cloth the main offence of his Moll Flanders. In this case, the manager, for reasons which are open to debate, wanted to have her arrested and charged, in spite of her pleas to argue that she never intended to steal, and that it was a mistake of his staff. But she wanted her pound of flesh and a few days later, a constable called at Jane's house. Wealthy women such as Aunt Jane obviously loved to go shopping and there was always a danger of such people being duped and exploited, often by a fabricated 'fitting up' of alleged theft and then a consequent attempt at blackmail.

On the fateful day of the incident, Aunt Jane went shopping at a place owned by Elizabeth Gregory, whose status was dubious, as the previous owner had run away while in debt who happened to be her brother-in-law. There was also the added scandal that Gregory had been living there with a man, Charles Filby, 'outside wedlock' which sent tongues wagging. It has since been established that Filby had a dark and troubled past too, being twice bankrupted while living in London.

The events of that day in the shop came out in detail at the trial. There was always going to be some uncertainty about what really happened, but the facts do point towards a scenario in which a regular (and very wealthy) customer was seen as good bait for a scam.

The trial took place at Taunton Castle in the Great Hall in March 1800. Presiding was Sir Soulden Lawrence, judge of the King's Bench, and contemporary of the great Lord Ellenborough while a student at Cambridge. He was knighted five years before this trial, and was to serve on the King's Bench for fourteen years. Accounts of him include a comment that his face 'denoted great acuteness and discrimination' and Lord Campbell said he was 'One of the best lawyers to have appeared in Westminster Hall in my time.' He had a reputation as being a man of great presence and also of great human insight and understanding. His talents were surely to be tried and tested by these courtroom spectacles, largely remarkably unusual because of the wealth and influence of James, and his vast sums of money spent on minimising his wife's chances of ending up being hanged or transported.

Elizabeth Gregory, who kept the shop in Bath Street, listed the people she employed – all of whom were present on the day of the alleged theft. Of the staff, a journeyman called Filby was to figure prominently in the tale. Jane had asked if some black lace, previously discussed, had arrived from London, and she was told that it had not come. As she conversed with Gregory, Mr Filby was measuring white lace on a frame by the door. Jane looked at some of a number of parcels of black lace, and then, when she said she would buy some, Filby was called over. He wrapped the goods, and as he did so, Gregory went downstairs to have her dinner, and Jane paid with a note: the lace she bought cost 19s and Filby recalled bringing her some change.

It was a quiet time of year, as Gregory told the court; on the counter there was very little in the way of goods displayed, so it was an easy task to see when items were passing. A short time after the purchase, as Jane and her husband were walking by across the street, Gregory went out to them and said, 'Pray madam, have you not a card of white lace as well as black?'

'No, I have not a bit of white lace about me,' Jane answered him.

'See in your pocket madam.'

'If I have then your young man must have put it in by mistake,' Jane insisted.

Gregory said that, as a folded packet was produced, Jane Leigh-Perrot went red and looked very disturbed. Sure enough, there was a card of black lace with some white also wrapped around. Jane said again that Filby had wrapped some white lace in the package by mistake, but Gregory said, 'No such thing… you stole it.' She turned to walk back, with the lace, to her shop, and Mr Leigh-Perrot came after her, saying, 'She did no such thing…' but Gregory then went to see the town magistrate. Two days passed before she could see him, as he had been away in Holland.

Filby was then called. He told the same tale, saying that he had been measuring the white lace and that he had left a shop mark on it as it was carded; so he was sure, having seen that same mark on the lace in Jane's possession, that she had stolen it. He only remembered wrapping the white lace for her. He said that he had turned his back on Jane to go to get her change, and then as he walked back, she had moved, and was standing by the black lace along the counter; he said that he saw her take her hand from the black lace.

Sarah Raines the other assistant confirmed this. The judge then addressed Jane and asked about her circumstances. Her reply has the measured tones of one of her niece's characters, as she explained that she was wealthy, and so had no motive for such a theft: that she was 'Left in possession of a fortune enough to gratify all her wishes in life.' She then added an impassioned plea:

> I know that my oath, in this case, is inadmissible, but I call upon that God whom you all adore, to attest that I am innocent of this charge and may he reward or punish me as I speak true or false…

There was an array of character witnesses, paid for by Mr Leigh-Perrot, including George Vansittart, the MP for Berkshire, who said that he had 'known the prisoner since the autumn of 1776 and for several years resided within a few miles of Mrs Leigh-Perrot…' and he 'conceived her to be a person of honourable and religious principles…' But a negative result could have been nothing less than the scaffold. The reason for this is that at the time, theft of items of a value over five shillings was a capital offence. In most cases, this was not given, but transportation to Australia for fourteen years was a more common sentence. The card of lace allegedly stolen was worth £1. But as was the case in so many instances, the 'genteel' and the rich were treated leniently. In fact, although she had to spend eight months in gaol until these March assizes, and that gaol was Ilchester, she was housed in the gaoler's lodgings.

Finally, at this trial in Taunton, she was acquitted. Although she was found innocent, it is obvious that the furore and scandal were going to present quite an ordeal to the Leigh-Perrot family. Within a month, the *Morning Chronicle*, after advertising the publication of the trail of a certain Thomas Shaw for fraud, added,

'Printed for West & Hughes, no. 40 Paternoster Row… of whom may be had *The Trial of Mrs Jane Leigh-Perrot,* price 1s.'

The story and trial have been widely discussed and the primary sources were all gathered together for one publication, *Jane Austen Family History* (in four volumes). But crime historians have been to work on the case and the consensus is that she was probably guilty. For one thing, the allegedly stolen lace was forced into the package in which Filby had put the other lace, and also it seems odd that after Filby had actually had the brazenness to try to blackmail the Leigh-Perrots, the four lawyers employed by the family did not go after him, keeping instead to the defence responding to the indictment. What has to be mentioned, though, is that Charles Filby was a man with a troubled past, having been twice bankrupt; and any man who could try blackmail in those circumstances has to be open to a level of cynical enquiry regarding his actions on the fateful day. In short, did he arrange it all – with everything planned to set up his victim? It seems very likely indeed that Jane's aunt was the victim of a scam: her wealth was the attraction, and the perpetrators knew that they had power if events allegedly happened in their own domain.

People were found who had shopped there previously and who stated that Filby had placed extra material in packages after they had made a purchase. The defence barristers went to great lengths to cast aspersions on the moral probity of Gregory as well as on Filby; the strenuous efforts made in this respect fall in line with general strategy in court at the time in which wealth and influence could override the legal process.

Students of the case tend to agree that the prosecution had a strong case. The usual question included in the judge's summing up, phrased as 'It is probable or reasonable for her to steal this lace?' tends to invite speculation with regard to the nature of shop-lifting by various wealthy celebrities in recent years, and to comment on why this happens. In other words, a variety of kleptomania may enter the discussion here, but of course, there was no such concept in 1799. It does not seem likely that there was anything of this nature in the case.

A likely explanation may lie in the back-story of this case; Jane, being a regular in the shopping precincts of Bath, and having plenty of time and money to indulge her display of status and social power, could easily offend the lower orders, and it could be that, as we know that she was in the same shop just the previous day, when she created a stir by being the quintessential 'awkward customer,' she may have made enemies, or even worse, if that habit was of long standing, she perhaps took one step too far and the 'tradespeople' were out for revenge. One is tempted to explain this in such a way, as the feeling of the attitudes taken, and the sheer determination on the part of the plaintiff to find a magistrate, smack of a vendetta. This was surely what lies behind the almost certain scam – sheer exploitation borne of an apparently manageable 'fitting up' of a woman who would have been at her ease, merely shopping in her local town, in one of her favourite shops.

For those eight months as she awaited trial, she was in Ilchester Gaol. Living with the gaoler must have been a hellish experience for a gentlewoman of great means and high social standing. She would have had to exist under conditions we now call 'house arrest' and that would have offered, as the most unpleasant experience, being in the midst of the noise, smells and potentially fatal diseases that were integral to prison life. In 1777 there were 74 prisoners there and most of these were debtors. Gaol fever was always likely to take a number of victims and of course the gaoler would bring the infections into his home. All accounts of the family of gaolers in the thirty years before the horrible regime of Mr Bridle, which cover the time Jane spent there, suggest that it was quite well run, but of course, for the upper-class 'special guest' prisoner waiting for her appearance at the assizes, the punishment was the shame, and that was to linger on.

The gaoler at the time was Edward Scadding, who succeeded his father Joseph, in the job. Edward was the eighth child in the family; he had been sent to London to train with the Goldsmith's Company, and was apprenticed there for seven years, before going to work in Bond Street. But his father died and the keeper's job back home was vacant. He married Martha Ward in 1782 and they were to have twelve children. He would have needed a large income and in fact he did very well: he earned £25 for the post, and on top of that prisoners paid fees to him. The discharge fee for debtors was 14s 4d; felons on release paid 6s 8d, and he was also paid for transport facilities at £3 12s each transaction. It has been calculated that his yearly income was around £55 without earnings from other commercial enterprise, as prisons at the time were places of a commercial nature; keepers expected to run businesses in the commodities needed by inmates, and of course, they had a monopoly.

Into this lively, noisy and populous family came Aunt Jane, along with her husband James, who stayed with her. There was a seven-month wait for the next assizes and the trial, and so her term in gaol was with the family as a prisoner, but a privileged one. Aunt Jane wrote letters and in these she gives a vivid account of life inside with the family. She wrote to her cousin Montague Cholmeley the following:

> ...this room joins to a room where all the children lie, and not Bedlam itself can be half so noisy, besides which, as not one particle of smoke goes up the chimney, except you leave a door or window open, I leave you to judge of the comfort I can enjoy in such a room... My dearest Perrot with his sweet composure adds to my philosophy; to be sure he bids fair to have his patience tried in every way he can...

One of the chief irritants in the prison life was that the children were everywhere, dirty and playful; Jane comments that her husband at one time felt 'small beer trickle down his sleeves on its way across the table... Mrs Scadding's knife, well licked to clean it from fried onions...' With a glance at the larger picture of life in gaols for prisoners awaiting trial for felonies, it has to be said that she had no idea how fortunate her wealth and status made her. She may have had unsavoury experiences and tut-tutted at the lack of order and hygiene, but many poorer people in her place would have succumbed to fever, debt or near-starvation behind bars.

We have to speculate whether or not she went shopping again in Bath. The scandal would have gone on and on, as the playwright Richard Sheridan described so well in his *The School for Scandal* of 1777, in which Mrs Candour says,

> ...the world is so censorious that no character escapes. Lord, now who would have suspected your friend Miss Prim of an indiscretion? Yet such is the ill nature of people that they say her uncle stopped her last week just as she was stepping into the York diligence with her dancing master...

In 1786, Hannah Carr stole 21s worth of printed cotton cloth from a shop. She was whipped and sent to a house of correction for two years. Her problem was that she was poor.

7

WILLIAM COMBE AND HIS FRIENDS

This is the sad tale of a writer who is almost totally forgotten today but whose life illustrates powerfully the precarious nature of creativity and the marketplace in an age of extremes of wealth and class status.

William Combe (1741–1823) has to be one of the most prolific and yet most forgotten writers in English literature. In the years between 1774 and 1800, before writing his 'big hit' *Dr Syntax*, he produced 50 published works, ranging from poetry to topography and from satirical works to history. He knew how to exploit topical subjects, such as his intriguingly titled *Letters of an Italian Nun and an English Gentleman* (1881) and how to cash in on scandals and 'issues' of the day, as in *Two Words of Counsel, and One of Comfort, to the Prince of Wales* (1795). Yet, in spite of all this literary activity, the chronicles of literature will not mention any of these early works with any note of importance. Combe, respected though he was by many in the *beau monde*, had a problem with money: he could not keep it and he kept on borrowing it.

By the time William Combe came to work with impresario and entrepreneur, Rudolph Ackermann and artist Thomas Rowlandson in 1809 to finish a project called *The Microcosm of London*, this jobbing writer was a guest of the King's Bench Prison and he had to return there at curfew. There must have been an affinity between the artist and the writer in this instance. Combe was 67 years old then and had crammed a great deal into his busy and eventful life as Rowlandson had done; but this rather maligned literary hack linked with the supreme satirist of Regency England was destined to produce a big hit – the true commercial success of both artists' lives.

Combe is a figure of paradox and contradiction and this was made more extreme by his unknown and uncertain years, and also by his sheer breadth of interests and publications. When he married Maria Foster, wife of a former school friend, in 1776, he was described in the press as, 'A gentleman who is universally known, from having distinguished himself in this, and other countries, in various shapes and characters.' He attended Eton College, and later after the death of his father he had a guardian called William Alexander, after whose death in 1762, he inherited considerable wealth from. There was something of the dreamer and the actor in him: he fancied himself as a gentleman among the dandies and rakes, and signed himself 'Esquire.' Yet he was in some ways entirely typical of the young men of his generation; like Rowlandson he travelled around France but was apparently penniless by 1770. His activities in the 1770s are a mystery: he may have been a soldier, and that never worked out, just as his earlier intention of having a legal career never worked out either.

What he did do well was make friendships and enter into a range of employment, developing himself as a jack of all trades. One close friend was the writer Laurence Sterne, author of *Tristram Shandy*; but by 1773 he had made his first venture into the lower reaches of the literary world, when he was given the chance to edit a book by Thomas Falkner called *A Description of Patagonia*. That was a common way into hack writing, just as Dr Johnson had done when he translated a work on Abyssinia (as it was then). After that there was no stopping him and with remarkable energy he wrote a play, *The Flattering Milliner*, which was staged in Bristol; what he did latch on to was the public's affection for parody. He wrote a volume of letters purporting to be written by Sterne to others, called *Letters to his Friends on Various Occasions*. Combe, the master of pastiche and copyist style, was born.

In the 1770s he was well known as an author despite the fact that his early books were anonymous. He was very much a journalist with an eye to topicality. In 1771 Henry Mackenzie published *The Man of Feeling* and it was a great success: it was no more than sketches of 'the new man' – one of refined sensibility and social grace. It had such an impact that it influenced various other writers including Charles Lamb. Richard Sheridan spoofed the whole notion in 1777 with his play, *The School for Scandal*. For Combe, it was there to be exploited and he wrote *The Philosopher in Bristol* (1775). It explains much about Combe that this was self-published: he was desperate to strike while the iron was hot, even though it meant a rash experiment financially.

The core of survival in the Regency years for any number of people in all walks of life was the desperate search for financial security, with a universal search for patronage and for other ways of surviving in the arts by any possible means. Combe was entirely typical in this. It was an age when, for instance, large numbers of people managed to live as sinecures and on pensions, doing very little. As a publication of 1819 called *The Extraordinary Red Book* shows, there were such posts as clerk to the dockyards, with pay of £100 per annum, along with thousands of pensioners such as Lady Collingwood who received £1,000 per annum and her two daughters each received £500 simply for being her companions. Crowds waited in levee for favours of the rich, scribes and hacks wrote letters begging for patronage, and a lower rank of hacks hung around the booksellers of St Paul's trying to live on pence for writing paragraphs, obituaries and reviews. Combe was one who tried patronage and when it failed, he ridiculed the rich instead. The Regent (George, later George IV) himself loved portraiture and if, like Thomas Lawrence, a painter could specialize in doing flattering portraits, then patronage might be more possible. But for people like Combes in the world, the printers and booksellers had the power, and with Combe in mind, it is worth noting that the writers generally did rather better than the painters in terms of the Regent's attention. As Donald Low put it:

…it made a difference to the social and intellectual climate that the Regent was as ready to talk with poets as with statesmen, and to confer a baronetcy on Walter Scott; in this way writers were made to feel that they counted for something in society.

In fact cash – the lack of it – became the formative influence on his life. Perhaps the stem of this was his debts related to the expense of keeping his wife in an asylum run by Stephen Casey at Plaistow in Essex. From the early 1780s he turned his attention to the easiest route to reputation in literature; he wrote satires. One of his targets was Simon Luttrell, Baron Irnham and later Earl of Carhampton. In 1744 he bought his country seat, Four Oaks, in Warwickshire, and by 1754 he was MP for Michael in Cornwall. Combe and others saw him as an excellent satirical target, and one ballad has him as a candidate for the title of King of Hell:

> But as he spoke there issued from the crowd
> Irnham the base, the cruel and the proud
> and eager cried, 'I boast superior claim
> To Hell's dark throne and Irnham is my name.'

His career up to meeting and working with artist Thomas Rowlandson was mixed, uncertain and risky; but one thing he did do which turned out to be successful was work with the new *Times* newspaper. When the writer and diarist Henry Crabb Robinson wrote his memoirs near the end of his long life (he died in 1867), he had known virtually everyone of any note in the Romantic literature and culture of the time, and he had known Combe earlier in his life when he was foreign editor and Combe was a regular contributor to what was then the *Daily Universal Register* which would become the *Times*. Robinson gives us his impression of Combe:

> I understand that he was a man of fortune when young, and travelled in Europe and even made a journey with Sterne; that he ran through his fortune, and took to literature, when house and land were gone and spent, and when his high connections ceased to be of service... I used to enjoy the anecdotes he told after dinner, until one day, when he had been very communicative, and I had sucked in all he related with a greedy

ear, Fraser said, laughing to Walter, 'Robinson, you see is quite a flat... he believes all that old Combe says.'

Robinson was embarrassed that he had been too credulous, but the tale tells us a lot about Combe when he was older. He clearly had been a minor celebrity in his time, and was still a good talker. But there was still the 'imitator' of old – that man who had written so much in imitation of others, for laughs and for satire, was later perhaps out of control in that respect and exaggerated everything for the sake of a good story.

Combe was 66 years old when he began his four year stint in prison. This was in 1808 and in that year, Ackermann needed a writer to handle the text for the last volume of the series, *The Microcosm of London*, to work with Rowlandson and his drawings, and Combe stepped in. Combe's biographer points out that the vast output that followed, writing that kept him busy behind bars and out on what we would today call licence, was not all hackwork. He writes:

> The compilation of seven hundred pages on Westminster Abbey... required a diligent search for information, and many volumes of antiquarian lore must have been brought to his quarters while he was performing this assignment. There was certainly a library in the Bench, yet Combe manages to cite learned authorities...

He definitely had a scholarly ability and he could cope with that as well as with real journeyman penny-a-line material. Between 1810 and 1822 he produced fourteen solid volumes of topography and contributed a massive amount of material to such publications as would give him column inches.

With all this in mind, it becomes clear that the man Rowlandson was asked to work with had known a brief period of fame and had moved in high circles. When Georgiana, future Duchess of Devonshire's brother George, wrote *An Epistle from a Young Lady of Quality Abroad to her Brother at School in England* in 1773, he was very much part of the vogue for supposed works by and about celebrities; William Combe pitched in, never one to miss a chance of some easy money. He produced *A Letter to Her Grace the Duchess of Devonshire* and *The Duchess of Devonshire's Cow: A Poem*. He was creating a set of fabrications when other supposed printed responses followed. 'Count Combe,' as he was known at the time, was on everyone's lips, at least for a few years.

Yet by c. 1810 he was in dire straits, and surely Rowlandson would have known his collaborator's past life history and felt some sympathy. After all, Combe had also figured prominently in other notable lives: his oldest friend was the painter and miniaturist, Richard Cosway, and when Richard died of a stroke as he rode in Regent's Park, it was Combe who helped the artist's sisters to settle their affairs. He wrote a memoir of Cosway and although it was incomplete, there are practical reasons for that, mainly a lack of materials sent by the friends and family.

Richard Cosway and his wife Maria had held salons in their home in Pall Mall, where they lived close to Gainsborough, and their circle of guests and friends included the Prince of Wales, the Duchess of Devonshire and Horace Walpole. He had produced a wonderful miniature of Mrs Fitzherbert, the Prince's mistress, and he had been welcomed into the royal coterie. Graham Reynolds, writing on Cosway, explains his success:

> Cosway achieved in his life many of the social ambitions which Joshua Reynolds had staked out for the artist. It is possible to fill out his biography with copious further incident and anecdote, for he was constantly in the public eye.

Such were Combe's contacts. He had been at school with Cosway and knew him very well indeed. It takes just a little conjecture to imagine William Combe being known and spoken of in all varieties of interlinking groups in the arts and in journalism during the Regency years.

Such was the man, now a debtor and prisoner, whom Ackermann found and signed up to work with Rowlandson. To really understand what Combe's life was like at this time we need to consider the debtor's life in the King's Bench at the turn of the eighteenth century. He was allowed out in the circumscribed area between stipulated times of the day. John Walter, proprietor of the *Times* in 1806, was the man who employed Henry Crabb Robinson, and we know from the latter's memoirs that Walter offered to pay Combe's debts. Robinson says of the matter,

> This he would not permit, as he did not acknowledge the equity of the claim for which he suffered imprisonment. He preferred living on an allowance from Walter, and was, he said, perfectly happy.

The King's Bench Prison was destroyed in 1780 by the destruction brought about by the Gordon Riots, and it became a grim landmark to all Londoners, having been there in Southwark, less than a mile from London Bridge, since the fourteenth century to the east of Borough High Street. The conditions inside always depended on what prisoners could gather by way of finances and although in 1754 reports had shown what an awful place it was, by the early nineteenth century, it was noted as a place where, if a small fee was paid, a prisoner could even be allowed to leave for a day or two. In Combe's case, the rules allowed him to live in the 'Liberties' – the area outside a borough where traditionally, freeman held customary rights. In an interesting sidelight on life in the Bench around 1800, Henry Angelo wrote in his memoirs of visiting a friend there,

> In the Bench... everybody knows that there is plenty of space to play at racket, which serves for an amusement as well as to improve the health. Often we mounted the top of the prison there... secure from being seen, and we played with the Highland broadswords.

Combe, because he still had work, had a small income. The idea was that creditors would wait until their debtor's circumstances changed and payments could be made to them. Obviously, if the debtor was thrown into a dark room and forgotten then nothing would ever be received from them. The debts Combe had were largely from Stephen Casey, the owner of the asylum in Plaistow where Combe's wife had been for years. But also he had been taking a small pension and that had been withdrawn, and the printer he worked for, Boydells, was in straitened circumstances. They had been paying him a retainer and that had to be reduced. As if all this were not enough, he had lived beyond his means. In 1790 he was living the life of an urban gentleman with a horse and servant, and as he loved the harpsichord, he bought a new one at the time, but on credit. By the late 1790s all these pressed on him. He had even owed cash to the painter George Romney, and we know that Combe wrote to Romney in 1798:

My dear Sir,
    I have called several times in Cavendish Square, & you were always at your villa – I have frequently designed to see you there in your rustic glory, but my engagements and the shortness of the days have prevented my enjoying that pleasure – It will not, however, be long before I shall take the opportunity to wait upon you, and to repay the obligation you were so very good as to confer upon.
    Your faithful and obliged humble servant
    Wm Combe.

This is clearly the voice of a man accustomed to the required ruses and excuses of a situation of severe debt; it is also from a man who lives on the edge of order and rationality.
    On 4 May 1799 the bailiff called, and a week or so later he stood in the court of the King's Bench; two men called Douglas and Lambert were suing for the sum of £40 11s 6d.
    Combe had some experience studying law and so had no attorney. He lost and so began a second term in gaol. Stephen Casey was pursuing him for a vast sum of almost £200 without costs.

In the King's Bench, though, he lived well. He was not a common debtor: he could eat and drink well. Tradesmen came into the prison each morning with food and materials; he would not have had to share a cell ('chum up' as it was called). Rowlandson and Pugin drew the Bench Prison in the *Microcosm of London* in 1809, showing the large panoramic sweep of its interior open ground and the throngs of people walking and talking, behind them the high walls and the blocks, made along the lines of what would be the new penitentiaries. The King's Bench Prison took its name from the court with which it was linked; what marked it out as unpleasant was the small size of the rooms. It was mainly a debtors' prison, as well as for prisoners kept there on religious crimes. It was a place where Catholic martyrs had met their fate. It was rebuilt not long before Combe was there, and the new version had 224 rooms, so it was massive compared with many of the other London prisons. Again it was destroyed in the Gordon Riots of 1780 and after that it was thought by many to be the prison with the best conditions in the city; wealthy prisoners could be quite at home there, almost as if they were merely experiencing bed and board at a lodging house.

Despite his freedom to walk out into town as long as he obeyed the curfew, Combe was obviously still in great difficulties. His situation was not to change; as Crabb Robinson explained in his diaries:

> At this time and down to the end of his life, he was an inhabitant of the King's Bench prison... I believe that Walter offered to release him from prison by paying his debts, which he would not permit.

This was John Walter, one of the founders of the *Times* who employed Combe. Combe was quite happy to continue as he was, merely existing with an allowance from Walter and tolerating his prison life.

The system of the 'day rules' at the prison was explained in a report in 1815. First there was the practice of 'chummage' and this meant that a man like Combe, who needed a cell to himself in order to work, could be free from a pad-mate if he paid, and then later, after serving time, he had more chance of keeping his independence. Then there were the 'rules of the Bench' which were obtained as a privilege. At the time of the report, of 440 prisoners, 220, Combe amongst them, benefitted from these rules: these covered a circumference of two and a half miles around the prison, and in that space a prisoner could live anywhere he chose, except in taverns, ale-houses and places of public entertainment. There was a payment and this is explained in the report:

> The Marshall, upon an application for his permission, takes security from the applicant, by way of indemnity for the debt with which they stand charged, and the purchase is made on the following terms: if the prisoner takes the debt of £100 or more, eight guineas is demanded for the bond stamp, and four guineas for every succeeding £100… if the debt be under £100, six or five guineas are demanded…

This all seems very rigid, but in fact there were plenty of cases in which people lived 'within the rules' and paid nothing at all to the marshall. The report concluded that the marshall sometimes used the rules to clear the prison.

Combe kept on writing and much of what he did was light and entertaining. In a work for Ackermann called *The Schoolmaster's Tour*, written for the periodical *The Poetical Magazine*, Rowlandson provided the prints; this was to become the work for which Combe was most celebrated and remembered: *The Tour of Doctor Syntax in Search of the Picturesque*, appearing in 1812. Combe's biographer wrote of this:

> For over a century it was to be a household favourite in many countries, and not merely for the celebrated aquatints which it was written to illustrate… The character of the absurd but somehow winning clergyman could not have caught the fancy of so many readers, however unsophisticated, had it not been

conceived with imagination and portrayed in the verses as well as in the prints with verve and originality.

In essence, Rowlandson and Combe were a very successful team. There was something of destiny, or at least, rare compatibility in these two men working together. Combe was born in Wood Street, in 1742, fourteen years before Rowlandson was to be born around the corner in Old Jewry; they were children of the same neck of London in Cheapside. They both had money troubles and both worked feverously to keep their heads above water; both were naturally suited to working to order from printers and other patrons, and of course, they relished the frisson of risk.

Combe was one of the most sociable of English writers. He appears to have known everyone on the literary and artistic scene of his time, and this extended from the early years of what was later to be seen as the Romantic Movement into the notoriety he came to know through *Dr Syntax*. When he did fall foul of the law and debt engulfed him, essentially, this lonely man who must have worked at his writing day and night for decades must have found prison life to a large extent quite amenable to his needs and habits.

8

MURDER AT THE LAMBS' HOUSE

Even in less enlightened times than our own, killers were not always sent to the gallows or to Van Dieman's Land. Sometimes they were sent to an asylum, and sometimes they were cared for and received genuine help. Sometimes they were abused and mistreated. There were factors involved that made these differences, and in the following story, these factors were highly unusual.

What John Dryden expressed in his couplet: 'Great minds to madness are near aligned, / And thin partitions do their bourns divide' invites a discussion of the link between creative writers and insanity. As Hanif Kureishi expressed it: 'Great literature is bursting with the mad; all important writers have wanted to engage with extreme states of mind...' That may or may not be true, but surely Charles Lamb, clerking in the India Office in London in the 1790s, would have given anything to be free of mental derangement in his home. He was to learn to live with it all his life.

On 21 September 1796, Mary Lamb, sister of essayist Charles Lamb, took a kitchen knife and plunged it into her mother's chest. Her father tried to intervene, and he was injured in the face. Charles rushed to the scene, saw blood on his father's face, and his mother lying dead on the floor. Mary had lost her reason, gone into a violent rage, and did something that horrifies any human society.

Charles, six days later, wrote to his best friend, the poet Samuel Taylor Coleridge, about the horrendous homicide. He expressed it plainly at first: 'My poor dear sister in a fit of insanity has been the death of her own mother.' Then he describes the aftermath:

> I was at hand only time enough to snatch the knife out of her grasp. She is at present in a mad house, from whence

I fear she must be moved to a hospital... My father was slightly wounded and I am left to take care of him and my aunt.

He coped well with matters, adding that he was 'calm and composed' and ready to 'do the best that remains to do.' From that moment, so he said, Charles would abandon 'vanities' such as writing poems and concentrate on caring for his sister.

This was a mania, inherited: Charles himself had also suffered not long before. The brother and sister who gave English literature *Tales from Shakespeare* and *The Essays of Elia* settled into a routine of care and preparation – for the damage and horror of insane episodes. When Mary's mania appeared, in its first stages, preparations were already made. The most vivid account we have of this comes from Barry Cornwall:

> Whenever the approach of one of Mary Lamb's fits of insanity was announced, by some irritability or change in manner, Lamb would take her, under his arm, to Hoxton Asylum. It was very affecting to see the young brother and his sister walking together (weeping together) on this painful errand; Mary herself, although sad, very conscious of the necessity for temporary separation from her only friend. They used to carry a straightjacket with them.

Had Mary not been in a loving and caring family, with some financial resources, she may well have been destined for Bethlehem Hospital ('Bedlam' in popular reference). But by the middle of the eighteenth century there were private 'mad houses' such as the one in St Albans, run by Nathaniel Cotton, to which the poet William Cowper went in his darkest, suicidal hours. At Hoxton there was the house run by the Miles family: their business at Hoxton House had started in 1695, and the Miles family took it over in 1715. In 1756, the first Jonathan Miles bought two large houses in the area and they expanded the concern. Then in 1782, the younger Jonathan Miles took over, and again expanded. He was eventually to be knighted and made a sheriff in 1806.

Hoxton House had one major problem, one common to many mad houses – it was overcrowded. The besetting sin of the private concerns was that of course they wanted to maximize profits and find room for as many clients as possible. They were to have severe problems in the twenty years following Mary's time there.

Of course, after the homicide of Mrs Lamb, there had to be legal proceedings on the matter. There was a coroner's inquest on 26 September, and the verdict and conclusions were summed up in a report in the *Morning Chronicle*:

> It seems the young lady had been once before, in her earlier years, deranged, from the harassing fatigues of too much business. As her carriage towards her mother was ever affectionate in the extreme, it is believed to the increased attentiveness, which her parents called for by day and night, is to be attributed the present insanity of this ill-fated young woman... The jury, of course, brought in a verdict, *lunacy*.

Charles himself had time at Hoxton, and he understood the nature of the illness, talking and writing about his 'lucid intervals' while in the asylum, such as the poem addressed to Mary, showing his insights, with the lines:

> If from my lips some angry accents fell,
> Peevish complaint or harsh reproof unkind,
> 'Twas but the error of a sickly mind,
> And troubled thoughts, clouding the purer well...

Charles insisted that Mary stay confined until their father died, and by the following April, that was the case. On 7 April she was taken from Hoxton and put into lodgings in Hackney. She had been confined for six months and Charles wrote in a letter:

> She boards herself. In one little half year's illness, and in such an illness of such a nature and of such consequences! To get her

out into the world again, with a prospect of her never being so ill again – this is to be ranked not among the common blessings of providence. May that merciful God make tender my heart, and make me as thankful as in my distress I was earnest in my prayers.

But a few years later she was ill again. They had moved to Chapel Street by then and the neighbourhood was obviously talking behind their backs. Charles wrote to Coleridge: 'My heart is quite sunk and I don't know where to look for relief. Mary will get better again, but her constantly being liable to such relapses is dreadful.'

At Hoxton, Mary was there before the problems started (due to overcrowding after it was used by the navy) and her treatment would have been of the more enlightened kind; traditionally, patients were subdued and restrained, and sometimes even beaten. But we know from the book written by Samuel Tuke of the famous Quaker Retreat in York, what enlightened treatment of the insane was. He stressed the importance of both moral and medical treatment. By 'moral' he meant engaging in functions of power and self-control, and interacting close-up, as was the case of George III when treated by Dr Williams, the Lincolnshire 'Mad Doctor' whose work in helping the King made the more enlightened methods more well known.

Mary was a manic depressive, extremely bipolar, and her violence was evident in her 'fits' or rages. Tuke, and Miles at Hoxton, were well aware of the benefits of attention to the general health, the use of cold baths for mania and warm baths for melancholia, and of diet. Central to the treatment was a healthy regime: 'We must not overlook the generally important considerations of diet, air and exercise,' he wrote in his book on The Retreat. The diet there was milk, bread, puddings, animal foods, cheese – with beer for men and tea for women. Moral treatment was at the core of the approach: efforts to confront behaviour and to use physical presence and dominance but not aggression or physical force, as was the accepted attitude in most places.

Perhaps the clearest insight into her phase as she moved into her mania was given by Coleridge when he wrote to his wife:

> I had purposed not to speak of Mary Lamb, but I had better write than tell it. The Thursday before last she met an old friend... The next day she smiled in an ominous way – on Sunday she told her brother she was getting bad, with great agony – on Tuesday morning she lay hold of me with violent agitation and talked wildly... there was not a moment to lose and I did not lose a moment, but went for a Hackney coach and took her to the private mad house at Hoxton... Charles is cut to the heart.

Mary Lamb lived to be 82. She died on 20 May 1847, outliving her brother by thirteen years. The diarist who knew William Combe, Henry Crabb Robinson, also knew the Lambs, was at the funeral, and wrote the following account of it:

> We drove to her dwelling, at St John's Wood, from whence two coaches accompanied the body to Edmonton... but the heat of the day rendered the drive oppressive. We took refreshment at the house where dear Charles Lamb died... There was no sadness. We all talked with warm affection of dear Mary Lamb...

Mary will be remembered for her *Tales from Shakespeare* – a book always in print. She worked on it mostly in 1806, and Charles explained her project to his friend in a letter: 'She is doing for Godwin's bookseller twenty of Shakespeare's plays, to be made into children's tales... I think it will be popular among the little people.' How right he was. Just four years after Mary's matricide, the government passed the Criminal Lunatics Act (1800). Rather than a mere domestic killing by a deranged person, this was the result of an attempt on the King's life.

On 15 May 1800, James Hadfield, a man who had served with the Duke of York in the European wars, stopped at a shop belonging to a Mr Harman in Greenhill's Rents, Smithfield, and talked about two pistols he had with him. He said that he had bought them for eight shillings and that he would clean them and sell them for a profit. He then left one of the guns in the shop, saying it might frighten his wife. He must have seemed a definite eccentric to Mr Harman, but he was not the only man who saw Hadfield on this day; in another shop he bought some gunpowder and spoke cryptically about 'a particular business' he had to see to on that day. He drank brandy and went on his way.

The particular business became clear to all present at Drury Lane theatre that night when Hadfield, terribly scarred on the face from his battle experience, stood on a bench, pointed a gun at King George III who had just arrived at the theatre, and fired. George had been responding to the cheers of the crowd, and the bullet missed him by about a foot, lodging in the plaster above him. This happened as the national anthem was being played. Within seconds, courtiers had covered the King and moved into protective positions. Hadfield was grabbed by several people, including two musicians, and dragged away, taken to the music room after being hurled over the rails of the orchestra pit.

James Hadfield saw the Duke of York, the King's son, approach, and said, 'God bless your Royal Highness, I like you very well, you are a good fellow. This is not the worst that is brewing.' As witnesses spoke at the trial in the hands of Lord Kenyon, it became increasingly clear that Hadfield was deranged. He had received his worst wounds in a fight near Lisle and had been so severely injured that he had been left for dead. It was known in some quarters that he had suffered mental problems since that day. In court, it appeared to the prosecution that he knew exactly what he was doing and had planned an assassination: after all, he had spoken to people en route to the theatre, and he had chosen the best spot in the place from which to fire at the Royal box.

The charge was treason, because the man had 'imagined the death of the King,' as the Treason Act stated. But Hadfield claimed that he had not planned to kill King George. There had to be testimony from two witnesses that he had planned an attempted the murder, because the offence was treason; but that also enabled him to have two lawyers defend him, and he was fortunate in having Thomas Erskine lead the defence. He was a very talented lawyer, the son of the Earl of Buchan; he had served in the navy, but he changed careers to study law and was admitted to Lincoln's Inn in 1775. He was called to the bar in 1778 and he made his reputation with his defence of Thomas Baillie who had published an attack on Lord Sandwich with regard to abuses in the government of the Greenwich Hospital.

But Erskine would have his work cut out with the Hadfield case. Luckily, some of the testimony, such as that by a Mr Wright, made it clear that Hadfield had been 'very confused and agitated' while standing on the bench. People nearby had assumed he was there because he wanted the best view of the King, but the facts seemed to be otherwise. However, it was Hadfield's behaviour in court that began to turn things in his favour. He had sat and stared into space, unconcerned that he was potentially going to be sentenced to be hanged, drawn and quartered. But it was the testimony of the Duke of York that turned the matter towards the issue of insanity. The Duke reported what had been said in the music room when the man had been restrained. He said that Hadfield had said he was 'tired of life' and that he 'only regretted the fate of the woman who would shortly be his wife.' What begins to emerge is a picture of a tough soldier who had, in the vocabulary of 2009, suffered 'post-traumatic stress disorder' and then other statements made it clear that all was not well in the accused's mind. For instance, Joseph Richardson said that Hadfield had said of the Duke of York, 'God bless him he is the soldier's friend and love!' and had said he had no desire to kill the King.

There had been a frenzy of shooting, though. Other bullets were found, one being in the box occupied by Lady Milner. At that point it must have seemed that, although Hadfield had done and said some very strange things, insanity was not really evident, and there had been rational planning of the act.

But then Erskine spoke. He focused on the question of intention: did Hadfield have a malicious intent to murder the King or was he governed by a 'miserable and melancholy insanity'? Erskine had the full biography of this tragically crazed ex-soldier; he said that Hadfield's real intention had been suicide on that night at the theatre, and that he had conceived the idea that if he fired near the King, he would be arrested and killed, so the suicide would be done in that way. He had thought of firing over the King's coach, for instance.

But then came the material on the personal life of the accused. Apparently, Erskine said, the man had tried to kill his own daughter just a few days before this attempted killing, and this was done because he thought 'his time had come and he did not want to leave the child behind.' Erskine had a long line of friends and military colleagues who then came to speak, and a full picture emerged of a mind unhinged. One soldier testifying said he had heard Hadfield say that he was King George, calling for a looking glass, and feeling for a crown on his head. Another man said that he had seen the accused 'in a paroxysm of madness' trying to kill him with a bayonet. Other army witnesses stated that Hadfield had been an ideal and excellent soldier before the fight at Lisle. This all was said of a man who had once been a royal orderly to the Duke – now a sad discharged soldier with horrible disfigurements and a profoundly disturbed state of mind.

The notion of insanity was therefore before the court. The succession of witness statements on that theme had persuaded Lord Kenyon that this was a man who was mentally insane, and he said that Hadfield could not be found guilty. His destiny was not a date with the axe or the rope, but a journey to Newgate and then to a London asylum, one at Hoxton kept by the Miles family, and then to Bethlehem Hospital, from where he would never emerge again into normal life.

The result of the Hadfield case was that, only four days after the trial, a bill was passed with the long title, 'A Bill for Regulating Trials for High Treason and Misprision of High Treason in Certain Cases, and For the Safe Custody of Insane Persons Charged with Offences.' The main part of this became the Criminal Lunatics Act of 1800. This established the idea of the lunatic being kept at His

Majesty's Pleasure. It required the detention of an insane person, the disposition being done without any work on the part of the judge: it was an automatic destination for men like Hadfield. Before this act, any person acquitted because of insanity simply walked free unless, as was the case with Mary Lamb, there were family members who would see to their medical provision. It was still a form of incarceration, but with a surface of 'home' material conditions rather than prison regimes. Hadfield, like Mary, went to Hoxton – rather than Bedlam.

Mary Lamb was a Hoxton patient because her family had enough money. Charles was not wealthy, but neither was he poor. Hadfield, in contrast, was indicative of a much large social malaise, tied up with wars and politics. Poor Mary, having no importance except to those who loved her, would have sunk into the hell of Bedlam if she had been alone or poor. Yet, with an eye to the Victorian future, at least Hadfield's case helped to bring about further enlightened legislation for the treatment of the insane. Charles Lamb coped heroically, and he had a number of friends to form what today we call a support network. In the end, it was affection and dedication that helped Mary survive. The private mad houses were certainly not all wonderful places, but Hoxton was what she and her brother needed, and their acceptance of their condition was nothing short of heroic. We can see the importance of the family support when we look at a case of 1790 in which an army officer ran amok in a Kensington palace apartment. He was captured and taken before a magistrate, who directed that he should be looked after until his identity was established: 'No bond could be given for his peaceable and good behaviour' so he was taken to Hoxton House.

The future lay in the formation of the great, large-scale asylums such as Broadmoor, which opened in 1863. By 1870 the population at that institution was 375 men and 100 females. An interesting comparison may be made with reference to the artist Richard Dadd, the paranoid schizophrenic, who similarly killed his father, on the evening of 28 August 1843, in Cobham Park. Dadd said later, 'Tell the great god Osiris that I have done the deed that is to set him free.' His destination was confinement in Bethlehem and then in Broadmoor. His story, in contrast to Mary's, shows the different effects of the more enlightened care of the mad as it developed in the later years of the century. The important contrast is that, without Charles, Mary may well have been one of the hundreds of insane people mixed in with the prison population across the land, whereas, even without family support, Dadd would most certainly have had the same post-trial destination as the one he actually had.

However, in spite of all Charles Lamb's pains and personal tragedy, the abiding image of him in literature is of the convivial friend, the essayist and good talker: the man who sat in the smoking room at the Salutation and Cat Tavern in Newgate Street, with Coleridge, smoking and drinking egg-hot (or eggnog as we know it now). It was a place where writers and men of letters met, as we know from an invitation to a dinner written by the stewards, called Cave and Bowyer, to a number of scribes:

> Sir,
> You are desired on Monday next to meet
> At Salutation tavern, Newgate Street.
> Supper will be on table just at eight
> One of St John's [Bowyer], t'other of St John's Gate [Cave]

In the end, an understanding of Lamb has to include, and try to understand, the two apparently contradictory images: that of him walking with Mary to Hoxton, his straitjacket under his arm, and that of Lamb full of jokes and merry tales in the coffee house. In some ways, that relates well to the commonly held belief that the best comedians and entertainers live with a deep sadness in their souls. He became known to the world as 'Elia' and his essays have been in print ever since the first edition such is the appeal of his light and playful humour.

9

GEORGE GISSING'S DANGEROUS LOVE

In 1850 the Belle Vue Prison opened for business in Manchester. Building begun in 1847 at a time when the prison system in England was moving slowly from old house correction facilities to large local prisons and penitentiaries. It was destined to be what today is called a dispersal prison: used for short-term prisoners mostly but also for those awaiting longer sentences, or at that time, waiting for transportation. The finished prison was like a castle, with buttressed walls and an iron-lined portcullis. It had four sections, one being for women and three for men. Each section had three tiers of cells and these were around an arched thoroughfare. In 1855 it was expanded, and the female section was then to house 250 women.

There were problems, as there were in all prisons – mainly of overcrowding and disease. In 1865 the surgeon wrote a report, and he referred to the death of a female inmate and added,

> I have for some time felt the want of a Dead House to which bodies could be removed from their cells, and in a case like this, fatal from a very contagious disease, it is very important that some provision be made.

Eleven years after that report, George Gissing, aged 18, was admitted as a prisoner, sentenced to one calendar month of hard labour. He was, in modern terms, a university student, and a very bright one at that. He had won numerous awards for his scholarship and had done very well financially. Everything pointed towards his move to Oxbridge and very probably to an academic life, perhaps with fellowships. But George, future novelist of the lower middle class strugglers in the

competitive and class-ridden society of Victorian Britain, had fallen
from grace, to the level of a common thief who had stolen from
his fellow students. A fellow could not sink much lower than that;
it defined him as a cad as well as a low criminal. Instead of wearing
a mortar board and gown, he now wore the coarse, arrowed livery
of Her Majesty's prison creatures, those who had dropped out of
society into the limbo of incarceration.

In 1948, George Orwell described the kind of writer Gissing
became:

> Gissing was not a writer of picaresque tales, or burlesques, or
> comedies, or political tracts: he was interested in individual
> human beings, and the fact that he can deal sympathetically
> with several different sets of motives, and makes a credible story
> out of the collision between them, makes him exceptional
> among English writers.

He adds that Gissing had seen and been among the working class, and
had regarded them as 'savages' but comments that he was only being
'intellectually honest.' As a prisoner in a local gaol, observing rules of
silence and working hard each day, he would have been among the
workers and those described at the time as the 'underclass.' And yes,
all that experience would have been 'material' for the future writer,
but he did not really use it, preferring instead to file the experience
away in darkness.

George Gissing was born in Wakefield in 1858, the son of a
pharmacist and town worthy: Thomas Gissing, a man who had also
published two slim volumes of poetry when young. His son clearly
inherited his determined character and thirst for knowledge. George
accompanied his father in naturalist study walks – a common
hobby in Victorian times, when all branches of natural science were
attracting amateurs and gentlemen, and collections of flora and fauna
were gracing the studies of men in the professional classes. George
went to school and excelled; it was obvious that he was of a scholarly
nature and that he should go to some place of higher education.

But Thomas died in 1870 and the best move was for George to work as an assistant teacher, earning so that his higher education could be funded. He went across to James Wood's School at Lindow Grove in Cheshire.

His schooling was to continue at Owens College, which moved into new premises and expanded (at Oxford Road) in 1873. His excellence as a scholar may be seen in his success in the exams for the University of London, which were open to anyone in the land. Anyone could attain a BA degree that way, and Gissing took the English and the Latin exams, and came first in the country. That success also earned him more money. His future was looking very bright indeed. But then he met a prostitute called Marianne Harrison, known as 'Nell.' The parallel is partly that of Hardy's novel of the student torn between high learning and sensuality, *Jude the Obscure*, but in this case, the scholar turned his life around from dedicated student to rake and wastrel – all in the name of love, for Nell became his 'eternal feminine,' as Goethe would have put it. Worship and adoration, and a dedication to saving her and redeeming her followed. Such was the first step on his path to ruin.

The college bordered on a slum area, and in that dark region of desperation and poverty, there were of course, houses of ill repute. Nell was a country girl from Shropshire. Gissing was smitten, gave her everything, and eventually had to steal from students in order to feed her greed for alcohol, and for anything else she asked for from her new 'protector' who ended up in the Irwell slums. The school authorities called in the police and money was 'planted' and an officer put on watch for the thief. Gissing was seen and caught red-handed. He was found guilty of stealing what in modern values would be £50.

In 1868, just before Gissing arrived in the city, Jerome Caminada, famous Manchester detective, started work there. He wrote in his memoirs of the kind of criminal cycle that the place engendered:

> We need shorter sentences, and we need to understand that as long as our system of punishment for the repression of crime is

accompanied by degradation it will foster the criminal spirit rather than remove it. Degradation strengthens evil propensities...

He also saw the slums which proved to be Gissing's doom:

The children who lived here were already following criminal pursuits, educated into them by hoary-headed, debauched, systematic trainers of the young. The young girls were already abandoned and reckless. The young men were already being set up for their life of crime...

Gissing was sentenced to his month of hard labour at Hyde and we know that he would have been set to work on the tread wheel every day, doing 100 hours in his time there. The wheel or 'mill' had been invented by William Cubitt in 1816, and fitted the new penitentiary ideal perfectly. The Select Committee on Penitentiary Houses of 1810–1811 had recommended that the government take over the task of making a national penitentiary at Millbank in London.

Very early in its history, a feature was published in the *Gentleman's Magazine* for 1822 explaining the virtues of this devilish conception:

Although but very recently introduced into practice, the effects of its discipline have, in every instance, proved highly useful in decreasing the number of commitments; as many prisoners have been known to declare that they would undergo any species of fatigue, or suffer any deprivation than return to the House of Correction, once released... The weight of a row of twenty persons is the moving power of the machine...

The same writer explained that in a gaol, where work was the main concern, the wheel provided 'everything necessary for grinding corn and dressing the flour...'

By 1835 a standard system of discipline and the 'silent system' were in force. Therefore, in the forty odd years before the creation of central government control of local prison with the Prison Act of 1877, prisoners in Hull were under the regime of tough work and the tread wheel (sometimes called the 'treadmill'). One newspaper in 1852 commented on the wheel: 'It is the best means for compelling the most refractory, indolent or sluggish prisoner to perform a fair, regular and profitable task.'

Gissing, along with other men of course, went to see Nell in her room in Water Street. He may have caught the romantic devotional attitudes so common in the aesthetics of his age, but he also caught herpes, and very likely also, syphilis. But Gissing was sure, as he wrote to his friend John Black, that he was in love with Nell. He said he had 'never felt so peculiar in his life' and that his 'head was swimming.' It had been a case of complete infatuation, and the couple had been away to Southport not long before the arrest. Clearly, both had felt a kind of exhilarating freedom: he from his loneliness and she from her squalid routine and mechanical sex for cash. The experience of Belle Vue must have had some kind of effect on Gissing as a writer. The real aim of a prison term then was the moral improvement of solitary reflection in a cell, with your own company. The lively, articulate scholar found that he was silent, and for what must have seemed an interminable period.

The penal philosophy behind this regime was explained by the supposed importance of silence. The rule of silence had to be enforced by severe punishments. The gaolers' journals across the country are packed with these types of entries: 'Confined Joseph Bailey in the dark cells for talking' and 'Confined Henry Oakes to his room for using thretnin [sic] prophane [sic] and abusive language to myself and Millin, the turnkey.' Women had the same rough treatment, as in the case of Mary Burrell in Maidstone: 'Confined to dark cell for three days on the report that she has used improper language.'

Reports on 'association' of prisoners – a term still used today – responded to the need for vigilance on the part of the staff, and in fact the records of gaols at this time are actually intelligence reports, because association meant potential trouble – even plans to damage property or attempt an escape. Association by day and by night was the subject of many reports, as in the following:

> The prisoners work in gangs of about twelve to twenty on treading wheels, at the capstan and in the manufactory... at night nearly the whole of the male population sleep in separate cells... The females work from eight to ten together in the wash-house and in gangs together on the treading-wheels. There are eighteen cells in which the females sleep single, the remainder sleep in cells with two or three others. The whole of the prisoners are under the constant supervision of the officers of the prison.

A month may not seem that long but with that kind of enforced silence and the vigilance and punishments involved, George's time inside must have seemed like a year.

As for Belle Vue Prison, it was declared unsafe in 1889 and it was given to auctioneers who sold the land for less than £5,000; the treadmills which George had helped to work were also sold off for £110.

This episode in the life of a very talented writer has to be balanced against the happiness he found later in life. As a successful novelist at the end of the century, George rubbed shoulders with such notables as Arthur Conan Doyle and H. G. Wells. In his own terms and by his own vision of life, he came to live well. We can only speculate on what torments from memory still worked on George as he enjoyed his new life, a very different person from that young man in his formative years in Manchester, loving, as Shakespeare's Othello says, 'Not wisely but too well.'

DICKENS' FATHER IN GAOL

There is a massive library of works devoted to the life of Charles Dickens in print, and every biography makes sure that the importance of one fact in the writer's early life is properly explained: the experience of the debtors' prison his feckless father, John, knew, and the implications of that on his son Charles. Prison life became one of the elements in his fiction that played a major part in the overall exploration of crime in the social life of Dickens' time: from Fagin and the pickpockets to Micawber the escaped convict. Dickens also made a point of getting to know the police, especially detectives, and behind all this interest laid the fact that his father had 'fallen' from respectability to ignominy, as so many of his contemporaries had done.

As Boyd Tonkin expressed it in an interview with Claire Tomalin, referring to her 2011 biography of the writer, 'We meet him in 1840, taking a break from his punishing routine to save a friendless servant girl with a dead infant from the gallows.' That is, his imagination and sensibility were inextricably bound with the criminality of his time, usually because that 'criminal' action was actually something that involved an unacceptable moral wrong which superseded the actual offence that was on the statute book. It helps in understanding the repercussions of his father's time in prison when we recall such matters which were so important to Dickens.

John Dickens only knew the debtors' prison, the Marshalsea, and that was fascinating to his son. But before any more detailed use of prison in his books, in *Sketches by Boz*, Dickens includes an account of a visit to Newgate and to the condemned cell. He writes:

> In the first apartment into which we were conducted… were
> five and twenty or thirty prisoners all under sentence of death,

awaiting the result of the recorder's report – men of all ages and appearances, from a hardened old offender… to a handsome boy not fourteen years old…

It was high drama: the recorder's report refers to the list of those condemned and those reprieved after the recorder of London had met with what was called 'the hanging committee' by some – the top legal minds and the Home Secretary.

In contrast, John Dickens' life inside would have been very different from Newgate in many respects. Under the Insolvent Debtors Act of 1813, a court was established for the relief of such people; they could petition the court for help. In John Dickens' case, there were various stipulations involved in this, and John Forster, Charles Dickens' first biographer, explains how this made young Charles suffer an extreme humiliation: 'One condition of the statute was that the wearing apparel and personal matters retained were not to exceed twenty pounds sterling in value.' He then quotes Charles' own words on what he had to do:

> It was necessary, as a matter of form, that the clothes I wore should be seen by the official appraiser. I had a half-holiday [from the blacking factory where he worked long hours] to enable me to call upon him… I recollect his coming out to look at me with his mouth full and a strong smell of beer upon him, and saying good naturedly that that would do…

John Dickens was unreliable with money and he had got himself deeper and deeper into trouble, as so many did then. The family, except for Charles, went into the gaol to be with him. It was only because he had the expectations of a large legacy that he could petition the Insolvent Debtors Court, and so this was a long process; he was therefore in the Marshalsea for three months. Finally, when released, he went with the family to be in the lodgings where young Charles had been staying with a Mrs Roylance.

The Marshalsea had been a prison since the fourteenth century and by the nineteenth century it had come to represent the quintessential nature of the large prison: a dual holding of one area for the poor debtors who lived in squalor, and a much better section for the more well-heeled debtors. As we have seen with the case of William Combe, prison life could go on for a very long time, so only with the legacy was John saved; without that he may well have been there for his life. In 1811 the old prison was abandoned and then rebuilt and the result was a prison within a prison, because it took smugglers and excise criminals, so the debtors were in more open areas whereas the real criminals were more confined.

Dickens describes this change:

> Itself a close and confined prison for debtors, it contained a much closer and more confined gaol for smugglers... incarcerated behind an iron-plated door, and a blind alley seven and a half yards wide.

Not long after John Dickens' stay there, it was amalgamated with other prisons in 1842 and the Marshalsea itself was demolished in 1897. The prison was by Borough High Street to the rear of St George's Church, and in Dickens' novel, *Little Dorrit*, we have wonderful confirmation of what is often said, that to a writer all life is 'material' and in this case it is so to a great extent. In passages such as this, where he describes the Marshalsea yard, we can see the results of observation and human sensibility:

> There was a string of people already straggling in, whom it was not difficult to identify... the shabbiness of these attendants upon shabbiness, the poverty of these insolvent waiters upon insolvency, was a sight to see. Such threadbare coats and trousers, such fusty gowns and shawls, such squashed hats and bonnets, such boots and shoes, such umbrellas and walking sticks never were seen in Rag Fair.

John Dickens was later once more behind bars, and on that occasion it was Charles who saved him, after borrowing money from friends.

But after that, something almost far worse happened: John sent begging letters to his son's friends. This embarrassing habit went on for years even after Charles had bought a cottage for his parents, hoping that at a distance, the humiliating begging would stop. As Dickens became wealthier and his circle of friends widened, his father must have seemed like a sad, irritating yet somehow fascinating survival from past miseries. Of course, Dickens made the most of his early suffering, and reflections on prison form part of that almost mythic body of work in his overall oeuvre of creative production, from his novels to his essays.

The impact of the prison experience within the family of course goes further and deeper than that. Prison has always been something that generates metaphorical thinking and may imprint on a writer's work an image from nightmare or a vision of an abstract insight into society. In the case of Dickens, there is no doubt that his father's time in the Marshalsea, and everything related to that, found a place in that area of the novelist's sensibility where he worked hard to interpret his times for readers both of his age and in posterity. Study of his novels, even at a cursory level, immediately locates an impressive series of interpretations of the zeitgeist of the mid-Victorian years and of the last years of the Regency. On the macroeconomic level, his society had causes and effects which tended to create social upheaval, mass poverty, the decline of trades and skills of a former age, and above all, a floating population of what came to be called the 'underclass.' Dickens dealt in the extremes of life and in the constant struggle for security and identity within that world of accelerated change. What more potent symbol of the loss of identity is there than that of the prison?

The prison extracts selfhood; in its walls, the prisoner feels his sense of identity slipping away as he is perceived as simply a 'number.' As a debtor, John Dickens, being on the 'master' side where the higher status prisoners lived, would have at least kept his clothes and basic possessions, and his family life would have gone on in a certain fashion. But basically, what he (and his son Charles) would have thought of as a stable life, with John working as a pay clerk for the navy, was taken away. A massive divisive assault by something called debt pulled the family apart. Dickens' on-going revisiting of his blacking factory work as a child provides something all writers know and value: an organising principle behind the words and the feelings as a narrative shapes itself in that pre-verbal form of the writer's imaginative centre.

John Dickens, a model for the great character Mr Micawber, died in 1851 after having surgery for a bladder disease. We have to admire the great writer's patience and humanity in repeatedly helping his wayward and profligate father; yet in terms of the writer's 'material,' the experience of prison created by John's debts, opened up themes for Dickens to explore through his imagination.

11

SAMUEL BAMFORD, THOMAS COOPER AND OTHER CHARTISTS

These writers were Chartists and so prison experience takes on quite another dimension. Among the ranks of these men who worked hard for political reform, there were many writers and poets, and most of these people saw the inside of a prison cell. In fact a great deal of our knowledge of the social history of prison life in this period comes from Chartist writings.

The Chartists wanted reform of the suffrage; the 1832 Reform Act had excluded those who were working with their hands in the toughest occupations that were making the Industrial Revolution possible; the Bradford Woolcombers were a significant part of that deprivation, and there was fertile ground for the demagogues and indeed for those who thought violence was the best way to achieve results.

The preparations for a full-scale confrontation with the forces of law had been on a terrifying level of agitation and fear, as the authorities saw it. In 1839, the wide space of Hartshead Moor, or Peep Green as it then was, was the scene of one of the largest Chartist rallies of the time. The area was like a fair, with over a hundred huts put up for the sale of food and drink. Some said that half a million people had turned up, but a more realistic figure was perhaps two hundred thousand. This was on 18 October and O'Connor was there, talking about the death of tyrants; another leader, Bussey, insisted that the best thing Bradford men could do was buy guns. Hartshead had been in use before, back in May 1837, when it staged a Poor Law meeting. It was fast becoming a spot in Bradford with a disturbing reputation for the local agencies of law.

Men did listen to Bussey and went to arm themselves. Justices of the Peace started taking depositions from shopkeepers who had had visits from desperate men out to use rifles; William Egan, a Bradford gunsmith, recalled how he had received visits from such locals. He stated, later as a witness:

> ...a person whom I did not know and who appeared to be in the capacity of a labourer called at my shop and asked me if I had any guns or bayonets by me, to which I answered that I had not.

Pressure was being exerted; men were desperate to arm and to take on the local authority. Egan said that in one period of about ten days, he 'had been applied to in order to alter muskets which have been brought to me without the stocks...'

Something nasty was brewing and the law employed spies – agents provocateurs – to infiltrate the radical activists. It was beginning to look as though Bradford would be the centre of a massive revolt of the excluded and oppressed people. James Harrison was an informer of this kind. In December 1839 he gave an account of what was going on with the extremists. He had been to a meeting at The Queen's Head, four miles from the city centre, and there he heard that there were around two hundred and sixty men armed and ready. There was also a London Chartist at this meeting and Harrison must have been worried. He recalled:

> In the bar there was this delegate, George Flinn, two men from the Queen's Head and myself. The man from London looked earnestly at me and asked Flinn if he knew me. Flinn said he had known me for three years and I was as good as any man in the room...

The magistrates were frightened, and wrote to the Home Secretary, expressing their concerns. These were E. C. Lister of Manningham, Matthew Thompson, H. W. Hird and W. R. Stansfield. They wrote about 'violent harangues of evil disposed and Revolutionary speakers' and they felt that 'some violent outrage' was about to take place.

What did actually happen in 1840? The leader of the abortive revolt was Robert Peddie, another Chartist writer, who is remembered for his autobiography and his narrative explains most things that took place. The plans of Peddie and his peers must have been terrifying to the place: Bradford then had a population of 66,000 and a police force of half a dozen men. There was no real police force outside London and these events took place only ten years after Peel's first Police Act. It is no wonder that localities relied on the army in these situations, and so naturally a bunch of ordinary labouring men would have no chance of success, and this was the case with Peddie's plans. James Harrison outlined Peddie's notions of a coordinated revolt, involving miners as well as the Bradford people. Harrison met with a group of insurgents at the Junction Tavern on Leeds New Road, and the plan was to go to Leeds and set fire to the magazine. Peddie's talk certainly included the desire to achieve the Chartists' aims – universal suffrage, no qualification for voting rights and so on. But there was another agenda, feeding other, nefarious discontents as well.

Everything was nipped in the bud; plans and leaders were known. Major General Charles Napier was given command of what was then called the Northern District in 1839. He soon had men billeted around the West Riding conurbation – for instance forty two men in Halifax in forty two houses; altogether in Yorkshire he had a thousand troops. He had to act quickly; very extreme things were happening such as a book in circulation in Halifax about facing barricades and how to face cavalry with a pike.

Peddie was given three years imprisonment after the Chartist Trials of March 1840. O'Connor had stolen the limelight and his trial was extremely protracted. In the end, no policemen were killed in the streets but this was soon to come, just eight years later. D. G. Wright has noted that Peddie's colourful radical career made him enemies on his side of the law too. Wright says that at one point 'the Scots Chartists decided they had had enough of this wilful, self-centred and histrionic man…'

Peddie wrote one of the most notable Chartist poems, in his book, *The Dungeon Harp* of 1844. He had this published at his own expense and he included letters and a copy of his petition to parliament concerning his situation. The frontispiece of his book has the words, 'Written during a cruel imprisonment of three years in the dungeons of Beverley' adding, 'a full proof of the perjury perpetrated against the author' and his epigraph reads:

Oh I tell how the brave oft have perished
But liberty never can die
It lives with the heart it has cherished,
'twill blossom and brighten on high...

His account of life in the house of correction includes a detailed narrative of his sufferings such as the episode when he was ill and said he could not work. He recounts this in the third person for a certain dramatic effect:

He was then, as before, locked up in the black hole, but in such a state of bodily distress that continued to increase to such an extent that he was compelled... to stretch himself upon the floor of his dungeon and make use of his clog for his pillow...

In his poems in *The Dungeon Harp*, Peddie writes a long lament on his loss of liberty and on the horrors of the prison, summed up in this quatrain:

The sound that greets mine ear
Is the doleful clank of chains;
Save when suffering Nature's groans, I hear
The wail of sorrows and pains.

When the Chartists went to prison, they caused trouble; Peddie at the Beverley House of Correction insisted on being treated as a 'political' and that was the main issue. There was also the case of William Martin. What has become known as the Sheffield Plot of 1840 involved Samuel Holberry, William Martin, Thomas Booker and others devising an attempted coup in Sheffield in which they planned to seize the town hall and the Fortune Inn, set fire to the magistrate's court, and then, linking with other Chartists, form an insurrection also in Nottingham and Rotherham. Their plot was betrayed by James Allen and Lord Howard the Lord Lieutenant, took immediate action. The result was that, at York Assizes on 22 March 1840, Holberry was sentenced to four years at Northallerton for seditious conspiracy: 'and at the expiration of that period to be bound himself in £50 and to find two sureties in ten shillings each, to keep the peace towards his Majesty's subjects.' He was leniently treated; under the Treason Act of 1351 he could have received life imprisonment.

The Chartists wanted electoral reform and mainly worked for votes for working men, along with the reform or electoral districts. In the years around 1840, the 'Physical Force' arm of that movement was accelerating and the Sheffield men were out to take extreme measures. William Martin was given a sentence of one year at Northallerton and he became such a problem that the issue reached parliament. His charge was seditious language and his behaviour in court tells us a great deal about the man. The *Times* reported:

On sentence being passed, he struck his hand on the front of the dock, saying, 'Well that will produce a revolution, if anything will.' He begged his Lordship not to send him to Northallerton, but to let him remain in the castle at York, saying that he was very comfortable, and having been seven months confined already was quite at home.

That was a certain way to open up the Northallerton sojourn, as the judges came down hard on Chartists and they would have had no consideration for these radicals' comfort. To Northallerton Martin went and there he was to stir things up. In court he had already stressed his Irish connections and made reference to Irish issues: he entered into 'a long harangue' on Orangemen, the King of Hanover and Rathcormac.

Martin refused to work on the treadmill as he had not been sentenced to hard labour and so such a punishment did not fall into that category. He was put into the refractory cell for that refusal, but his case was supported by the Secretary of State, Lord Normanby, who wrote that

> ...the prisoner, who was not sentenced to hard labour, cannot legally be placed upon the wheel against his consent... and that if he should refuse to labour upon the wheel, it would be illegal for the gaoler to place him in solitary confinement.

But a visiting magistrate argued against this by quoting one of Peel's recent Gaol Acts which allowed for the work done on a treadmill to be defined as either hard labour or as 'employment for those who are required by law to work for their maintenance...'

Martin, as far as we know, was compelled to work on the mill, and he claimed savage treatment at the hands of the Northallerton staff:

> One morning as soon as I had left my cell, the Governor's son... took me by the collar and dragged me from the place where I stood and threw me with violence against the wall, and on the following day he told me I must expect different treatment from what I received in York and he added that men had been reduced to mere skeletons when their term of imprisonment expired and that it should be the case with me...

With Samuel Bamford's story, we have a witness to events who was then a famous radical activist and is now one of the most celebrated Lancashire working-class heroes from those tough days of the struggle for rights for the ordinary people. He was also a talented writer, mostly in autobiography and poetry. Bamford was a prisoner in Lincoln Castle in 1820, sentenced for his part in Peterloo. In his classic book,

Passages in the Life of a Radical, he has left a picture of Lincoln Prison at this time, and he also tells the tale of two men, Booth and Parrish. In Peterloo Fields, Manchester, ordinary people had been cut down and killed by hussars while attending a meeting there. Bamford must have been a bitter man when he came into the gaol and he was to see many other gaols during his tempestuous life.

Bamford saw Cobb Hall, at the corner of Lincoln Castle, and in March, 1821 he saw the gallows waiting for these two men. Mr Justice Richardson had led the trial of the two, who had burgled the house of an old woman in Whaplode. Parrish who had been a shepherd to Mrs Cully, wrote to the men he had met in Lancashire, and Bamford explains why that connection was there:

> It was a custom… for harvest men to go from Lancashire to Lincolnshire – a 'cwokin' as they called it – and a party of these from Astley Bridge had been in the habit of doing the harvest work…

Bamford notes that the robbers went to the farm dressed as mummers, and then 'The robbers next tied the inmates fast and plundered the house of about nine hundred pounds worth of plate, money and notes…'

Although they had been masked, one had fallen off and the man was seen: that was Booth and so he was soon tracked down. Bamford wrote that 'The hounds of the law soon laid on the true scent and set off for Lancashire with the speed but not the noise of bloodhounds.' Some Lancashire men had fled across the sea, but in the end, the shepherd and Booth were in court and sentenced to hang.

The events leading to their deaths were seen by Bamford who described the scene:

> It was rather a cloudy and gusty morning when, getting up to my window, I beheld the gallows fixed, and two halters ready noosed, swinging in the wind. To me, this first sight of the instrument of death was both melancholy and awful… I placed

myself on the rampart leading to the tower, on which stood the gallows, and had a full view of the criminals as they crossed the green. First came the Governor, bearing a white wand; then some halberdiers and other sheriff's men, then the deputy sheriff, next came the criminal, then the chaplain, the turnkey, the executioner and assistant... and other javelin men...

The Lancashire man also saw the two felons die: 'The shepherd appeared to have his eyes fixed on the instrument of death from the moment he came in view of it' and 'He appeared faint and required assistance to mount the ascent.' Booth, wearing a blue coat, was 'more dogged in his manner' and 'He held his head a little on one side, gave a glance at the gallows, spat out some white froth... and went on again without help.' The bodies were removed 'on the backs of men' after they had been left hanging there for an hour. They were laid side by side on the floor of the town hall.

Chartist writers were many and had varied talents. As well as Bamford, there were, notably, Thomas Cooper and Gerald Massey. Gerald Massey was widely known as 'The Chartist Poet' in late Victorian society, and was still alive after the turn of the century, dying in 1907. The writer James Milne knew him in old age and at that time he had turned to ancient Egypt as the focus of his creative attention. Milne quotes one of the later poems, in his memoir, and adds, 'That is not sung by the Chartist poet of the day when the railings were pulled down in Hyde park and the great Duke of Wellington's windows were broken by the hungry populace' and we can see by that remark why so many of Massey's peers were destined for prison terms. His fame rests perhaps in the fact that he was the model for Felix Holt in George Eliot's novel of that name, and Milne adds, 'He was in youth "a spirit that can stand alone"' and he was respected by many writers in the 1890s when Milne wrote.

Of all the Chartist writers, Cooper is the one who has most explained prison life. After a life of moving from place to place, as teacher and journalist, Cooper was working for the *Leicestershire Mercury* when, in 1840, he attended a Chartist meeting in Leicester, at which shoemaker

John Mason spoke. Cooper himself had the skills of a cobbler, a trade he had pursued while reading and absorbing a massive amount of knowledge. Mason had a powerful effect on Cooper, who until that time had dreamed of being a writer, and he had worked with Edward Bulwer Lytton in his electioneering to take Lincoln as a Liberal.

He had begun to see the reasons why Chartism was fired by such pressing concerns, when he saw at close hand the stockingers of Leicester and started to understand the plight of the un-franchised and marginalized working people of the land. After the Chartist meeting he walked and saw the stocking weavers working late; he asked some basic questions on domestic economics and his passionate and energetic nature was stirred into a resolve to do something. He had been politicized. Only a short time before he had taken a romance novel he was working on to show the novelist Bulwer Lytton, and his response had been tepid and indifferent. Discouraged as a writer, Cooper now turned his considerable powers of communication to the service of the Chartists.

By 1842 he was becoming increasingly involved in what is called 'Physical Force Chartism' – a frame of mind linked forever with the demagogue Feargus O'Connor. But Cooper, being a strong individual, developed what came to be called the Shakespearean Brigade of Leicester Chartists' and he was referred to as a 'general.' He had become a leading figure in the movement and in 1842 he went to the important Manchester Conference. He was being noticed by government spies.

The focus of activity moved to Hanley, and there his crowd-pleasing skills and fiery speeches played their part in an arson attack. He was arrested and charged. So began his life as a prisoner; he did time at Stafford Prison, and in his autobiography, we have a vivid and impressive picture of a writer locked up and fighting for his rights. In prison, he was to write the work for which he is best remembered, *The Purgatory of Suicides*, and later came his life-writing; he lived to be 87 years old.

The battle for rights in prison is a powerful story. After his sentence of two years, he was told that he could not have books and writing materials, so he started a campaign against the prison authorities to have things changed – and also to be properly fed.

At one point he did something that today would have given him a long prison sentence: he assaulted the prison chaplain in an attempt to be noticed and to demand his rights to education and a good diet for work. As he wrote in his autobiography, his aim was to 'break down the system of restraint in Stafford Gaol, and win the privilege of reading and writing, or end my life in the struggle.'

The conditions were very harsh: there was a straw bed and two rugs, and the daily food ration consisted of a little bad meat, old bread and 'skilly' – the standard prison porridge. But he was fortunate in finding other prisoners who were able to obtain writing materials so he produced a petition to be put to parliament, and the governor was tolerant enough to allow it. The petition worked and he was allowed what he wanted. He relates the situation of his writing life inside at that time, when he was not sure if he would be free again to work:

> During the first two months I not only could not get at my books, but I had locked up the only copy I possessed of the hundred lines written as a blank verse commencement of my purposed poem... As I could not recover them, and did not know if they would ever yield to allow me the use of my books and papers, I thought I could defeat their purpose by composing and retaining the poem in my mind... So my thoughts were very much intent on making a new beginning.

Cooper was a dedicated scholar as well as a writer. Not only did he complete his poem and the romance he had shown Bulwer-Lytton while in Stafford, but the authorities realised that they could drag him out of political militancy by offering him the chance of a university education, which he declined, sticking to his principles.

On 4 May 1845, he was released from Stafford and set off for London, his writings in his bag, ready for a new chapter in his busy and dramatic life as writer, speaker and Chartist leader.

12

BROTHERS INSIDE

Today we live in a world in which public figures may be the subject of quite cruel, excessive and merciless satire, and the authors of these attacks escape unharmed. It was not always so and the Regency years in England provide a clear example of when such activities were very risky.

This tale begins with a prison, the scene of the main narrative. In 1860, documentary writers Henry Mayhew and John Binny wrote an account of the Surrey Gaol at Horsemonger Lane:

> We approach the Surry Detentional prison by a narrow lane, leading from the bustling thoroughfare of Stone's End. It is enclosed with a dingy brick wall, which almost screens it from the public eye. We enter the gateway of the flat-roofed building at the entrance of the prison, on one side of which is the governor's office, and an apartment occupied by the gate warder, and on the other is a staircase leading up to a gloomy chamber, containing the scaffold on which many a wretched criminal has been consigned to public execution.

Nothing much seems to have changed at the gaol since 1813, when writer and editor Leigh Hunt was led inside to serve a two-year term for seditious libel.

The writer's misery began when he and his brother, John, published in their periodical, the *Examiner*, some words which were aimed at the Prince Regent, later George IV. The offensive phrasing was that the 'Adonis in loveliness' was 'a corpulent man of fifty' and 'a violater of his word, a libertine over head and ears in disgrace, a despiser of domestic ties, the companion of gamblers and demireps.' This came as a riposte to a piece printed in the *Morning Post* after there had been a toast to the Prince at a political dinner in London at which His Highness had been praised as 'Protector of the Arts' and as the 'Glory of his People.'

Attacking the Prince was nothing new. In fact, as historian Vic Gatrell put it,

> Princely and aristocratic profligacy was not new to this era. What was new, thanks to expanding print cultures and markets, was its high visibility... No sexual adventurer suffered more from this exposure than the Prince of Wales.

That was back in the late 1780s, so assaults on the man's behaviour and morals were nothing new when the Hunts made their satirical remarks. From the last decades of the eighteenth century, the print culture had generated prints commenting wickedly on the private affairs of the high and mighty. The genre of caricature was also extremely popular, and magazines and cartoons were devoted to that new and entertaining form of popular art. The print shops around the Strand and St Paul's Church in Covent Garden were packed with satirical prints.

By the time the Hunts started their literary and political publication, things had changed in terms of politics, mainly due to the effects of the French Revolution and the state's fear of anarchy in the streets in England. In 1812, when the libellous remarks were printed, England was at a very low ebb: there was extreme poverty and deprivation across the land as the Industrial Revolution was underway; the Luddite risings in the north were challenging technical and managerial change with violence; there was a war with America in progress; and the Home Secretary was employing agents provocateurs to spy on the activities of all kinds of radicals.

There is no doubt with this context in mind that the authorities were out to teach a lesson to those young men who were using their pens to join in the general expressions of dissatisfaction and complaint against all areas of political misdemeanour, and against individuals whose morals were in question. The Hunt brothers had started their periodical in an exciting atmosphere in which a variety of radical clubs were meeting, theorizing and publishing material with regard to new and challenging ideas of equality and fairness in the mechanisms of power. The brothers were to experience the wrath of the state in its mood of repression; they found themselves in court before Lord Ellenborough on 2 December 1812 at the Court of King's Bench. They were defended by Henry Brougham, afterwards Lord Brougham, who at the time was working to have a place in parliament while also making a good reputation at the bar. He had defended them a few years earlier when the government was hounding them after publishing attacks on the extreme punishments of military flogging. On that occasion, the young lawyer was victorious and won an acquittal, but now, before the trial there was an attempt to stifle the Hunts' satire by means of offering a compromise: if they promised not to write anything satirical against the state, they would be spared prison. They were determined to stand trial, though, and Ellenborough was waiting, understanding the task of his court.

Lord Ellenborough was Edward Law from Cumberland; he was admitted to Lincoln's Inn in 1769 and took the silks in 1787. Famously, he defended Warren Hastings and won an acquittal after five years of the trial process. Later, when Sir Samuel Romilly was working to mitigate the severity of the criminal law, he opposed that campaign, and made it clear that he was for extreme punishments and keeping the law hard and relentless against criminals, secure in the belief that the 'Bloody Code' of over 200 capital punishments was acceptable. An early biography of him notes that 'Though the bigotry of his opinions as a legislator incurred grave censure, in his character as a judge he won the admiration of all.' But that statement would not have been agreed upon by John and Leigh Hunt.

The sentence was that they would have to go to separate prisons for two years and also pay a fine of £500, with the additional proviso that, even at the end of their stretch, they still had to find £500 each as security for future good behaviour. Off they went, straight from court: Leigh to Horsemonger Land and John to Coldbath Fields.

In his later autobiography, Leigh records the impact of his arrival:

> The sight of the prison gate and the high wall was a dreary business. I thought of my horseback and the downs at Brighton; but congratulated myself, at all events, that I had come thither with a god conscience.

The warder, Ives, expressed a wish that he would have given a hundred pounds to see Hunt elsewhere than in his care, and said he wondered why the government had sent Leigh there because, as he put it, 'the prison was not a prison fit for a gentleman.'

Leigh wrote a series of letters from prison and in one of the first he described his room, 'the highest and farthest room on the right hand… as you face the western side of the quadrangle,' a room he was soon moved from to a situation of comfort and elbow-room: the prison doctor had him moved to two rooms to the south of the infirmary. As may be seen on a plan provided by Mayhew in 1860, the infirmary is separate from the main prison buildings, and this clearly reveals just how spacious the area was. In short, Hunt received special treatment. There was even better news to follow, when his family came to join him. Essentially, although by many he was seen as a martyr to his beliefs and to the cause of press freedom, really almost everything in life was preserved, except for the fact that he was locked up.

On 16 March his family arrived and the place was domesticated. One biographer noted that 'His larger room, disguised with wallpaper and distemper, became a bower of roses under a Florentine heaven; the bower of course sheltered a pianoforte, a lute and busts of the great poets…' Leigh's journal of his life inside includes an account of this new comfort, and writes as if addressing his children:

> My feelings have been pleasanter since moving; partly owing to this change, but principally to a good fit of my illness, which

I had yesterday, and which always helps me in the end... My literary pursuits will make a principal figure in this journal...

Indeed they did, because while in gaol, Hunt was extremely productive. He read voraciously and started work on a long poem which eventually became *The Story of Rimini*.

It has to be said that this poem has suffered some criticism and a certain degree of ridicule. In the collection of 'bad verse' entitled *The Stuffed Owl* first published in 1930, the editors, Wyndham Lewis and Charles Lee, add this anecdote to their account of Hunt:

> Perhaps Theodire Hook summed up the whole poem not inaccurately when he fathered on Byron the observation:
> O crimini!
> What a nimini-pimini
> Story of Rimini!

The poet Tom Moore had written a poem for Leigh on his imprisonment, and the spirit of this was actually near the truth of what the prison stay was like:

> Some beam that enters, trembling as if awed,
> To tell how gay the young world smiles abroad!
> Yet go – for thoughts, as blessed as the air
> Of spring or summer flowers, await you there.

He had good company. He wrote in his autobiography that visitors could stay with him until ten o'clock at night, and then 'the under-turnkey, a young man with a lantern... came to see them out.' He added that Charles and Mary Lamb came to see him 'in all weathers' and also Lord Byron arrived. He was affable on the surface, but he wrote to Tom Moore:

> Hunt's letter is probably the exact piece of vulgar coxcombry you might expect from his situation. He is a good man, with

some poetical elements in his chaos, but spoilt by the Christ Church hospital and a Sunday newspaper – to say nothing of the Surrey gaol, which conceited him into a martyr.

His brother John was ensconced at Coldbath Fields in Clerkenwell. This had been built in 1794 and had 232 cells. In their poem, *The Devil's Thoughts*, Southey and Coleridge had written:

As he went through Cold Bath Fields he saw
A solitary cell;
And the Devil was pleased, for it gave him a hint
For improving his prisons in hell.

Twenty years later, the governor of Coldbath Fields Prison in London, G. L. Chesterton, was drawn to support a newly conceived silent system imposed at Auburn Prison in New York and reported on by William Crawford. This was a zero tolerance approach, based on the authorities' belief that any kind of group gathering or opportunity to discuss dissent was the first step towards riots in the streets. After all, in 1780, the Gordon Riots had shown what could happen if the mob took the chance to indulge in some anarchy in the streets. They had caused terrible damage in London, even the Fleet and King's Bench Prisons had been ravaged in the rampage.

When Governor G. L. Chesterton approached Coldbath Fields Gaol in 1827 he was astonished: 'As the yard was approached, the ear was assailed with a discordant buzz of voices, occasional singing and whistling, and ever and anon an interjectional shrick.' He was soon to change all that. Later, when the Select Committee on Gaols and Houses of Correction reported on its findings,

Entire separation, except during the hours of labour and religious worship is absolutely necessary for preventing contamination, and for a proper system of prison discipline silence to be enforced...

Chesterton, at Coldbath Fields, wrote about the beginnings of the new rules:

> On the 29th December, 1834, a population of 914 prisoners were suddenly apprized that all communication by word, gesture or sign was prohibited and, without a murmur, or the least symptom of overt opposition, the silent system became the established rule of the prison.

At any time in history, a prison regime will reflect the criminality and lawlessness of the time; in the 'long eighteenth century' the outstanding crimes were murder and other offences against the person, as well as damage to property. It was the age in which capitalism expanded and new businesses flourished. But the laissez-faire thought of the age of entrepreneurs also brings with it the need to protect property.

We know a lot about Governor Chesterton because a French writer called Flora Tristan visited Coldbath Fields Gaol in 1839 and met the governor. Her account of him shows how remarkable he was:

> The Governor, Mr Chesterton, is a very distinguished man; he speaks Spanish and French with equal facility… everything about him proclaims the man dedicated to the service of his fellow men… The prison is clearly the mainspring of his life and he regards the prisoners as his family; he knows nearly all of them by their first names.

Flora found his rules hard though, saying, 'They prescribe rules of perpetual silence and solitary confinement for the slightest infraction.' Her explanation of the silent system is one of the clearest we have:

> Under no pretext may the prisoner address either his fellows or the warders. If a visitor ask him a question he must on no account reply; only when he is ill is he permitted to speak…

Then he is immediately taken to the infirmary… any prisoner who breaks the silence is severely punished.

But in 1813, John Hunt was in reasonably tolerable circumstances, as by that time the rules were primarily for petty offenders; it was the Middlesex house of correction for men, the female equivalent was at Tothill Fields. John's situation was surprising, when it is considered that in 1818 almost four thousand people were committed there, and that the greatest number there at any one time was 472; the labour undertaken there at the time was in white-washing, carpentry and bricklaying. The gaol had played its part in one of the most notorious crimes in the whole of the nineteenth century, just a year before John Hunt arrived, because the murderer involved in the Radcliffe Highway Murders of 1811, John Williams, left this world, his body carried on a cart to the top of Cannon Street, where it was ignominiously heaped into a prepared hole.

On 5 February 1815, an announcement in the *Examiner* told readers that the editors had left their prison cells. John Keats celebrated the event by writing his poem, 'Written on the Day that Mr Leigh Hunt Left Prison' in which he wrote that his friend saw more than the prison walls – 'In Spenser's halls he strayed, and bowers fair/ Culling enchanted flowers…' Certainly for Leigh Hunt, unlike so many in these chapters, prison experience had had its virtues. He had found and used good writers' material. It doesn't really matter that the product of his stay, *The Story of Rimini*, has not exactly attained the level of a classic; Hunt will always be a part of the literature of the Romantic period, but principally as an editor and polemicist rather than a creative spirit at any estimable level.

13

THE CRIMES CLUB: CONAN DOYLE AND CHURTON COLLINS

Arguably, the most well-known image of the fascination with crime in the late Victorian period comes from the iconic figure of Sherlock Holmes and the arrival of the *Strand Magazine*. The concept of this new publication came from George Newnes, who wanted a British magazine with a picture on every page. The editor received two stories from Arthur Conan Doyle: *A Scandal in Bohemia* and *The Red-Headed League*, and his excitement at reading them led to the employment of Sidney Paget to provide accompanying illustrations. A massively influential literary creation was born. Holmes was not only an amateur forensic student but also a meticulous preserver of criminal profiles and biographies, and that cultivation of an interest in the deviancies of his world made him entirely representative of a trend amongst men of letters at the time. 'True crime,' as we would call it in the twenty-first century, was becoming something worthy of serious attention.

In addition to the Holmes stories, the *Strand* carried features such as 'Smugglers' Devices' and 'Her Majesty's Judges' and a little later, the *Harmsworth* magazine went even further into this market, having a similar format to the *Strand*, but having even more curious and fascinating criminal topics such as 'Poison Devices: Conceived by the Grim and Ghastly Ingenuity of our Forefathers' and 'The Medical Detective and His Work.' The magazine succeeded *Harmsworth*'s very popular 1887 publication, *Answers to Correspondents on Everything under the Sun*. By the mid-1890s, perhaps due to the advent of the Whitechapel murders, interest in all things criminal had burgeoned in the mind of the reading public.

Literary men who also had professional lives in other areas – notably in medicine and in administration or academia – began to bring their criminal studies into their club lives. One of the most typical men of this group was John Churton Collins, a man whose life was as puzzling as his intellectual interests, in some ways, and of all the subjects of these essays, he is perhaps the man most actively in pursuit of criminal acquaintances.

On 12 October 1908, The Classical Association held its annual business meeting, and it was announced that Professor John Churton Collins was scheduled to read a paper on 'Greek as a Factor in Popular Education,' but then his death was announced. A few weeks before, his body had been found in a ditch near Lowestoft and the inquest returned a verdict of accidental death. His son wrote in his memoir of the scholar that his 'lonely and premature death remains, and always will remain, terrible to those who miss him sorely.' He was accustomed to the lecture hall and the deadlines of his literary productions: a week's work in 1897 included a review of a new work on Virgil, a lecture on Tennyson in Richmond, two lectures at Wimbledon on Elizabeth I, and a lecture at Hayward's Heath on the *Iliad*.

Churton Collins represents that bookman of the late Victorian years who expressed opinions on a broad range of topics, from a solid base of wide reading, firm opinions and a sound university education. He graduated from Balliol in 1872 and began a career of busy and committed discourse on books of all kinds. In his life, there was always an essay to be written, a book to review and a lecture to give. But he also excelled in the *conversazione* and the club. After his busy week of lectures listed above, he attended a dinner party with Sidney Lee and other literary men. He came to maturity in the 1890s when periodicals such as the *Idler*, edited by Robert Barr and Jerome K. Jerome, catered for the growing readership of literary opinion; there was a hunger for debate, informed discussion and educated reviews. Autodidacts (such as Leonard Bast in *Howard's End*) found this climate of opinion and reverence for books suited their temperament and Churton Collins became well respected – a professor who had the common touch – and he shone in the world of university extension lectures.

Yet this was not all; the law and crime seemed to dog him all his life; in 1888 he was at a house on Torrington Square when thieves broke in and he had property stolen: two pistols and an overcoat. The pistols hint at another dimension to the man perhaps. Then in 1899 he was in court in the libel case of Yeatman v. Harris, after reviewing a work on Shakespeare by John Pym Yeatman for Harris' *Saturday Review*. In the dock, Collins was accused of having a 'clique of barristers behind him' and questions were asked as to his qualifications for reviewing such a work. He sensibly admitted that he was not able to read and understand some of the sources used, but 'He had sufficient learning to criticise the book' as the press reported on the events at the Queen's Bench.

It should come as no surprise, then, that Collins was a member of the Crimes Club. He had developed an interest in contemporary crime before he mixed with Sir Arthur Conan Doyle and other leading lights of that society. The club was first discussed at a dinner given by Henry Brodribb Irving, son of Sir Henry, in 1903, and it was properly conceived the following year at the Carlton Club. The plan was to have dinners throughout the year, and members would speak on criminal topics; apart from Conan Doyle, members included Fletcher Robinson, A. E. W. Mason and George R. Sims.

For Collins, the attraction of criminal mysteries was perhaps akin to that of interpreting texts and ascertaining the intentions of authors, at a time when books were written and lectures given in the manner of the 'life and work' tradition, as if literary intentions were plainly explicable. At a deeper level, the interest in criminology, in its amateur version as it existed then, was also concerned with human motivation and the darker side of human nature. He was always open to communal and open discussion on every aspect of humanity: in 1904 he was one of the founding members of the Ethological Society, whose aims were to study human nature 'Not through any one department of science, but taking from all the different branches the most practical and useful to arrive at a knowledge of the intellect and character of man...' as the *Times* reported.

He not only read the journals and the law reports, but was active in the search for experience of what the great Scottish crime writer William Roughead called 'the criminous.' Collins delighted in meeting and interviewing criminals when he had the chance and his curiosity led him into correspondence with some of them.

In 1897, for instance, he went to meet the infamous Tichborne claimant. This was the case of an impostor called Arthur Orton. The heir to the Tichborne Estate was shipwrecked and drowned in 1854, but then in 1865 a butcher from Wagga Wagga in Australia started to claim the title and behave as if he was in fact the proper heir. He was eventually tried for perjury and the famous judge Henry Hawkins, Lord Brampton, prosecuted for the Crown. Orton was sentenced to fourteen years hard labour, was released from Dartmoor in 1884 and survived until 1888. It was at this time that Collins knew him. The perjury trial had lasted for 188 days and Judge Hawkins wrote in his memoirs, 'I did what I could to shorten the proceedings. My opening speech was confined to six days, as compared with twenty-eight on the other side.'

In his notes after meeting the claimant, he wrote: 'His voice was soft with a curious mixture of accent, partly cultivated and that a little overdone, and partly vulgar.' Collins had a correspondence with the claimant, and this traces the decline of the impostor. He wrote to Collins in one of his last letters:

> My illness prevents me going out. On Thursday my wife gave a music lesson and earned a shilling, and that is all we have to live on… If you could only spare a shilling or two for our immediate wants, I should be very grateful. Having no means of getting a stamp my wife has kindly consented to walk down with this in the hopes of finding you at home…

Four months later, the claimant was dead.

Of course, the case of Jack the Ripper absorbed his interest too, and in April 1905 he went with members of the Crimes Club to all the scenes and sites of the murders. He listened with attention and fascination to the account given by Dr Gordon Browne of the post-mortems done on the Ripper victims.

But if we look for the origin of Collins' interest in true crime, the case in question is the Ireland's Eye mystery of 1852. Collins' son wrote that his father had always been interested in the study of crime and criminals, but that in 1891 he bought a publication on the trial of William Burke Kirwan, the man convicted for the murder of his wife in the 1852 case. So intrigued was he by the case that he suggested to Mary Braddon that she use the story as 'material' for a novel; she replied that Collins should write the story: 'Your own pen, I am convinced – as a logician and profound thinker – would be much more effective in rehabilitating this unhappy man.'

The fact is that Collins did indeed try very hard to gather more information about the mysterious death of Kirwan's wife, Maria. William Kirwan had been married to Maria for twelve years in 1852, when they set foot on Ireland's Eye for the day. But he had also had his mistress, Mary Kenny, in the village of Sandymount, just a little way south of Dublin. It appears that the two women knew that they had to share the man almost from start of the marriage in 1840. By the end of that day, Maria was found dead, in suspicious circumstances, and Kirwan was destined to be charged and convicted of her murder.

William lived by his trade: when he was not earning from art directly, he was an anatomical draughtsman. In Merrion Square, close to the centre of Dublin just a few streets from the Dáil, was the parliament house. He lived among medical men, and they were always in need of such skills. The example of George Stubbs, the famous painter of horses who studied anatomy in depth shows this: his friend Dr Atkinson in York found him work in drawing for anatomical studies. Artists had traditionally been assistants to surgeons, as was the case with the great surgeon, John Hunter, who had an artist called Bell as his assistant; Hunter had issued a ten-year contract with Bell for him to draw the contents of the surgeon's special collection of medical items. He even paid Bell to write a catalogue of specimens a little later. An anatomical draughtsman was paradoxically a talented dogsbody in some places: though he had exceptional skill he was not seen as a 'proper' painter.

It is not hard to imagine this artist, a man trying to keep his business alive in one of the smarter areas of the city, while spending time with Mary as well as with Maria. What emerges is a double life – something common in the middle-class Victorian world in which a mistress was often a family acquisition little different from a horse or a servant. Here was a man struggling to keep his head above water, an ironical metaphor, given his destiny. He was clearly increasingly desperate once his family with Mary grew apace: by 1852 he had seven children by her.

Money did not flow freely; aspirations were high. William had married into a little money and certainly had a status above the norm. But when Maria's body was brought in from the island, gossip was about insurance money. Yet the topic was never raised by the prosecution. For many it was a working-class crime – insuring the lives of relatives who would die mysteriously. Just six years after this death, a case in Liverpool was found to be a systematic poisoning of a whole family for insurance profits.

We have a man living with a 'front' of the respectability of Merrion Square yet with a family tucked away just down the road. He is a man in need of finance, a man with a false face shown to the world. His landlord in Sandymount was a Mr Bridgeford and he said in court:

> Mr Kirwan lived in one of the four houses in Spafield of which I am the landlord. He resided there for about four years. I saw a woman there whom I always supposed to be his wife. I saw children in the house. I have notes from the woman and I think she signed herself Theresa…

This was Mary Kenny, her full name being Theresa Mary Frances Kelly. The Kirwans were not so poor that they could not afford a servant: Catherine Byrne lived in the house as a maid and she told the court that there were seven children and that Kirwan was often there for long periods in the day, and often he stayed the night.

William Kirwan, then, was a man with one foot in respectable and bohemian Dublin, a man to find being sociable at parties or alone in the early hours being melancholic; the other foot was in the dangerous underworld of crime and fear along the bay by the South Wall. Was he a man who longed for the thrill, the challenge, the pump of adrenaline?

One writer in 1853 gave us a picture of William:

> Mr Kirwan is a little above forty, a native of Mayo… He is tall and well-looking, strongly built, and the expression of his countenance, firmness, corresponds with his strong limbs, broad chest and duly-proportioned body.

The writer knew him and commented that he was admired as an anatomical artist 'from which he realised a handsome income.' Yet he would have had to be vastly wealthy to support so many and two households' rent.

An artist who was reasonably well-off then, but with an obstacle to further success which he had to remove. It makes no sense; he and Maria had taken lodging for the summer at Howth and they often went out to Ireland's Eye. He had no reason to kill her. That was lost in the supposition and legal bungling. Collins wanted to know more, and in 1891, after reading an account of the case, he wrote to some of the best legal minds in Ireland. It was forty years after the case, but one man, Walter Boyd, had some strong opinions. By 1885 he had risen to be a judge, and had been admitted to the bar in 1856, while the Kirwan case was fresh in the minds of Dubliners. He was a QC by the Hilary term in 1877 and had learned his trade on the north-east circuit. Boyd found himself in retirement, the recipient of questions from Collins and their correspondence, though it offers nothing conclusive about Kirwan's guilt or otherwise, but instead says a lot about Collins.

John Gross, in *The Rise and Fall of the Man of Letters*, opines that Collins, after the Merton Professorship of English Language and Literature had been established at Oxford in 1885, was passed over and was not happy about it. Gross writes that Collins was 'a hustler, a trouble-maker' and he had a bad name, being seen as 'a kind of intellectual cabaret turn.' That exuberant, expressive and provocative side of him was exactly what would have made him a successful barrister in some ways; now here was a literary man in search of a new thesis, solving a criminal mystery rather than a question of literary authorship or the trickier bits of the Linear B text in the Anglo-Saxon studies his beloved Oxford would have appreciated.

Collins' letters to Boyd and also to the former prison surgeon who had known Kirwan brought out some stunning statements, such as 'Kirwan refused to produce evidence for the defence as he said he could not be convicted...' and Boyd's assertion that he had no doubt about 'the religious element, having had much to say to the hostility displayed toward Kirwan, but I think it would be publicly undesirable to mention the fact.' Kirwan had been sentenced to hang and was later reprieved, and Boyd wrote to Collins to say that he was,

> Greatly struck at the time of the reprieve by a remark by Kirwan when I visited him in prison. He said, 'If they believe me to be guilty why don't they hang me?' I thought a guilty man would not have said so, as he would have been only too glad to escape with his life.

Churton Collins exemplifies the kind of involvement in what we now call 'true crime' that the writers and critics of the late Victorian period had enjoyed; theories and opinions on current or recent 'horrible murders' reported in the Penny Dreadfuls was partly a development of what De Quincey had in mind in his richly ironical treatment of murder as a 'fine art' in his essay dealing with Williams of the Ratcliffe Highway murders, and other Georgian horrors. The periodicals of the last two decades of the nineteenth century were eager to feed the public curiosity for such things as 'criminal types' or the work of the lawyers and the police. Literary men weighed in with their interest and a niche for the more profound and informed discussion of matters of murder was established. The Crimes Club certainly took off and was transformed. Ingleby Oddie, a founding member, was disappointed when the chat and entertainment became a version of literary criminology.

With this in mind, it is surely time to appreciate Churton Collins for playing a major role in that strange but fascinating corner in the massive hall of literary culture in which 'criminous' topics were allowed into serious discussion, rather than being left in the ghetto of the true crime magazines. The inheritor of that tradition today is arguably Richard Whittington-Egan, a writer equally at home when narrating the life of Richard le Gallienne as in explaining the enigma of the Great Torso Murders.

14

IRISH WRITER MEETS WIFE KILLER

As a prologue to the case of Wilde, a glance at a book written by Arthur Griffiths, published just a few years before Wilde was in Reading Gaol, is of interest. Griffiths published *Secrets of the Prison House* in 1894 and in this he has a chapter called 'Some Gentlemen Gaol-Birds.' He writes:

> At times, but happily rarely, a man of high culture and upright character makes a short sojourn within the walls... I have seen one of this class who spent twenty months in a prison chamber; it was always gaol for him, although he was allowed all possible relaxation of discipline; daily visits from his wife, permission to wear his own clothes, to provide his own food, to exercise alone, and to such amusements as were within his reach...

This is a rare insight into the flexibility and humanity of the system, as it had been reorganised after legislation in 1865 and 1877. Wilde was in a similar situation, but was not quite so lucky.

Griffiths understood the special situation of these inmates, who were totally in a different classification from common criminals, and he showed great understanding; he comments on one such case:

> To see this poor, broken, humiliated man in convict garb, cut off from friends, permitted to see his wife but once a month, condemned to unlovely, uncongenial toil... must satisfy the sternest vindicator of the law that the way of transgressors is hard.

A better reflection on the fate of writers and similar 'gentlemen prisoners' would be hard to find.

The first part of this story concerns a man known as Captain Slack around the Holmes, one of the poorest places in Doncaster in the 1860s, with mission churches and schools. When the story first broke, the press fastened onto the fact that Slack and his wife were both 'of intemperate habits' and that appears to have been the source of the man's murderous rages, this particular one proving to be the killing of his wife and his own ruin.

On 11 July, around six o'clock, Thomas Slack, aged forty, came home from a long drinking session; he found his wife Ann also drunk. They lived at the Holmes in Wheatley. A little girl had been helping Ann do some housework and she left just before Thomas appeared on the scene. The house had a kitchen and a front room, and later it was ascertained where exactly Slack struck – for he did strike, just minutes after coming home. He went into a rage when seeing her drunk: he took out his pocket knife and stabbed her in the neck. Ann staggered outside, screaming for help. She was bleeding heavily, of course, and she fell as she went outside, into the arms of a neighbour who had rushed to the spot.

The woman who first held the dying woman was Hannah Slack, (aunt by marriage to the prisoner) and she left Ann, breathing her last breath, with another woman before going inside and confronting the man.

Hannah found him in the front room sitting on a sofa with his hand in his pocket and she said, 'You have murdered your wife!'

Slack answered, 'I have not seen her, where is she?' But the drunk strangely then added, 'Oh is she dead? She was my best friend... I'm very sorry.'

Hannah Slack emerged as the heroine in the tale. The hand in his pocket grasped his knife and he said that he was going to take his own life. Hannah restrained him and shouted for help. It was very risky for her to have gone in there alone in the first place. The other neighbours around responded and finally came to her assistance. Slack was grabbed and held, and a short time after the police arrived, led by Superintendent Astwood, who arrested Slack and took him away. He was charged with murder but he was sober enough to say that it was not so, because he was in drink. That was significant, because at court he stood indicted on charges of both murder and manslaughter.

The definition of murder needs to be placed at this point in the sad story: a murder is a killing with is done 'with malice aforethought' – there has to be a *mens rea* – an aim to kill – and then the *actus reus* – the deed done which would lead to the taking of life. The two Latin terms are crucially important. Slack had immediately thought that his drunkenness would be a defence and would pre-empt a murder charge. He was wrong.

Dr Charles Fenton gave medical evidence, saying he arrived on the scene about forty five minutes after the deadly attack. He found wounds two inches long on Ann's neck; this was close to the left ear and death had been caused by the piercing of the carotid artery.

It was clear from this that the knife wound had caused the death.

It was looking bleak for Slack. His defence, Mr Price QC, straightaway introduced the notion of provocation, saying,

> I have known and worked with the family for several years…
> Mr Slack is a good and kind husband. The deceased was very
> unkind and provoking in every sense of the word. She did not
> bear a good character.

Price then launched into the high drama of the plea aimed at the jury, insisting that this had not been wilful murder. He said, cleverly, that 'the law was bound to lay down general principles, but the application of these principles lay with the jury…' In other words, he was angling for the wilful murder to be dropped by reason of severe provocation. The argument was that Price had suffered long and hard over the years, worthily trying to bring this fallen woman back to habits of sobriety.

But Hannah Slack's testimony was crucially important. Slack had some barges in the River Don, hence his nickname, and Hannah pointed out that he was often away from home; their marriage was a very unhappy one, she said. Then she described how she had seen both of them very drunk on that fateful evening. After the killing but before Hannah had known, she saw Slack walking along the garden and he 'doubled up his hands and ruffled his hair in quite a delirious manner.'

Price was stretching all sinews and brain cells to paint a good picture of Slack. He cross-examined Hannah and she explained,

> he has had to call me up dozens of times when he could not get deceased to bed because she was so drunk… I have often seen men come to the house when he has been away.

The tale of their life together was depressing. Hannah pointed out that when the Slacks were first married they had a well-furnished house. 'Drink had led Ann to pawn absolutely everything for beer or gin-money,' and Hannah pointed out that there was not even a blanket in the house to put over the deceased's body.

It was apparent that the man had been driven to distraction, and the presiding judge, Mr Justice Lowe, asked Price if he intended to set up an insanity defence. The answer was no: he was keeping to the provocation appeal.

The Slacks had been married for ten years, but for the last six months the decline had been extreme. Hannah said that Slack had been going to Sheffield almost every day in that period and coming home drunk, finding yet more items pawned and both of them heading for complete destitution.

This story could have been just another domestic homicide, at a time when such things were happening all the time. Slack's story would have faded into oblivion, but fate decreed that he was to meet Michael Davitt, writer, journalist and politician, born in County Mayo in 1846. After being evicted from their land, his family moved across the Irish Sea to Lancashire, where Michael found work in a cotton mill, and at the age of eleven in 1857, he lost an arm in a mill accident.

Slack had completed seven years of his sentence and was in Dartmoor, when along came Davitt, and they met and talked. Slack told him that after a year in gaol his brother wrote to him advising hope and patience. Then six years past. Davitt and Slack had the following conversation:

'And have you not heard from your brother these six years?' I asked, after listening to his story of drink, murder and repentance. 'Oh no,' he replied, 'Did not he say I need not expect to have a letter again until he could send a good one? I am expecting one now every day, and I think that as I have served seven years the Secretary of State will send me my release, coming on Christmas.'

Slack was then taken to another prison and Davitt did not see him for another five years; then he was brought back from Portsmouth and davit asked the same question. Slack replied, 'As I have done twelve years now without a report, I am certain the Secretary of State will soon discharge me.' Davitt concluded that if the 'wretch' was ever told of his brother's conduct, he would have been 'released by death' before he had served half his term.

Davitt took a profound interest in prisoners and in prison reform, and he was a literate, widely-read man. As was the case with many nationalism Irish prisoners in the nineteenth century, he wanted books and thirsted for learning, as well as to write poetry and autobiography. When John Mitchel, another Irish writer who wrote a famous prison journal, settled into prison life, he lamented the low quality of the prison reading-matter:

As for the books I read... The literature most in favour here seems to be of the very paltriest of London novels reprinted in America and they have those vile compositions called family Libraries... dry skeletons of dead knowledge...

Davitt also searched for good reading, and being a writer, he searched for and cultivated other writers. He met several poets, one of which had a staggering level of egotism. Davitt begins his tale: 'It was while studying the backs of doors and the bottoms of dinner-cans that

I first met a convict poet in the flesh.' He gave the Irish writer a poem to criticize and Davitt adds, after gaining possession of the man's slate (there was no paper),

> I became possessed of his slate and found about fifty lines of a medley which commenced with 'when we are most alone we are least alone' containing nothing but unconnected lines stolen from Milton, Shakespeare and Young's *Night Thoughts*.

But Davitt is important for many reasons, and one of these is his realisation that writing and reading poetry in prison life is very important. He wrote a guide to reform in his second volume of memoirs and in that he had a lot to say on the use of the Free Libraries in prisons. He argued for more use to be made of libraries within prisons, and in fact developed a range of suggestions, all expressed with the practical eye of a man who had been at the receiving end of a prison regime.

Davitt was a man of many parts, and a great thinker: his later writings reveal an impressive sensibility, and his prison memoirs make it clear that he genuinely felt for others, with a real empathic sense of their troubles and the injustice around him. His writings on his prison time urge one to speculate as to what achievements he might have had as a reformer on questions of social issues, had he not been so busy with politics, as in his opposition to Parnell and his advocacy of non-denominational education. These activities made him enemies, but then, he was used to that, and in some ways thrived on it.

15

OSCAR WILDE, WILDE SENIOR
AND READING GAOL

Oscar Wilde is arguably the most notorious literary prisoner in English literature, closely followed by John Bunyan. In his writing he had a lot to say about the prison regime in Britain at the end of the nineteenth century, and in his *Ballad of Reading Gaol*, he produced a classic of prison poetry.

In his essay, *De Profundis*, he wrote:

> While I was in Wandsworth prison I longed to die. It was my one desire. When after two months in the infirmary I was transferred here [to Reading] and found myself growing gradually better in physical health, I was filled with rage. I determined to commit suicide on the very day on which I left prison. After a time that evil mood passed away…

We know now, thanks to the research of Anthony Stokes, who is a senior prison officer at HMP Reading today, why conditions improved for Wilde in Reading. But he had had a terrible time.

Wilde's fall and disgrace are well known. His homosexual relationship with Lord Alfred Douglas, the son of the Marquis of Queensberry, led to a bitter confrontation with the Marquis, and eventually Wilde was in court, first after he took out proceedings against the Marquis for criminal libel (libel today) and then, after losing that action, he himself was charged with sodomy. He was found guilty and was sentenced to two years in prison; that was on 25 May 1895. First, he spent the weekend in Newgate and then was taken by cab to Pentonville. So began his degradation. By the time he was moved to Reading Gaol he had experienced the worst of the prison system as it was at that time. Entry meant a strip search, followed by a medical examination and a bath; then he would have put on the prison clothes, with the black arrows, signifying that he was now no more than a chattel belonging to her Majesty's government.

From the beginning, Wilde had problems with the food, and he became ill, suffering from diarrhoea. He could never really sleep properly either; he was a large man and the bed was no more than a board, with one blanket. It was difficult to be warm at any time. But he was, in some sense, a celebrity prisoner and he had friends in high places: one such was no less than R. B. Haldane, who was a prison commissioner. Haldane took an interest in Wilde's case from the start. In June 1895 he visited Wilde and promised that he would have books, pen and ink. Such a thing was forbidden, but as events were to prove, there were many aspects of Wilde's prison life that involved breaking the rules.

There was a furore on the part of the governor, but as is still the case today, there are exceptional circumstances in prison, and matters may vary according to who the person is and what their condition may be. In Wilde's case, part of the reason for him having special treatment was that he was seriously ill. Deaths in prison are always embarrassing for the staff as well as for the prison service and the Home Secretary. With Haldane's help Wilde had his books – fifteen altogether. Later he was to work in the prison library and that was one of the most humane moves made on the part of the authorities.

He was moved to Wandsworth in August 1895 and there his condition deteriorated even more: as already noted, there was where he wanted to die. Concern was expressed for his mental health and a doctor was sent to look at him, along with some specialists from Broadmoor. It was decided that he was not mentally ill, but the Wandsworth period did nothing but harm to the public image of the man whose plays had once entertained the glitterati of London. A chaplain wrote to the newspapers to report on the fact that, while having an interview with Wilde, he had smelled semen. In the late 1890s, the time when the intellectuals were full of talk about the 'degeneration' of the human race, it was one of the worst things to happen to the man who was already, in the public opinion, the epitome of everything that was repulsive to the heterosexual, empire-building commuter class, with its mediocre and philistine views on high art as well as on moral stricture.

But Wilde was soon transferred to reading, and there, as Anthony Stokes has discovered in his book, *Pit of Shame*, Wilde had friends who made his time inside much easier. But in Reading there was an execution during Wilde's time there: a soldier called Wooldridge, of the Royal Horse Guards, had murdered his wife. Wilde's experience of seeing the man, and in fact, of even seeing the burial after the hanging, within the prison grounds, gave us the classic poem, *The Ballad of Reading Gaol*, in which we have the lines:

> I walked with other souls in pain,
> Within another ring,
> And was wondering if the man had done
> A great or little thing,
> When a voice behind me whispered low,
> 'That fellow's got to swing.'

This reminds us that the spell in Reading was far from paradise. However there was a man on the panel of prison visitors who was instrumental in alleviating some of the pain of prison life for the great writer. We now know from Stokes' research that George W. Palmer, of Huntley and Palmer, the biscuit manufacturer, was one of the prison visitors. At that time they were known as the Board of Visitors, whereas today they are the Independent Monitoring Board, and their role is to tour their allotted prison and enquire on conditions by speaking to prisoners in the daily routine. The Palmer's biscuit factory was next door to Reading Gaol, and so Haldane's aim of looking after Oscar Wilde took another course, as well as being a source of books and paper.

There was another link between the Palmers and Wilde: just a few years before the trial, Wilde had been a visitor at the home of Palmer's younger brother, Walter, whose wife was a lady who liked to run a literary salon of a kind: Wilde had been to the biscuit factory in 1892 and signed the visitors' book. But there was also another measure taken to make Wilde's time at reading more palatable; the first governor had been a strict disciplinarian, and had no time for rules being bent or broken, so he was promoted to another prison, and the new governor, Major Nelson, was far more sympathetic to Wilde's condition. That move was followed by the appointment of a warder called Martin, and he would become something of a special friend – again, something that would not normally be tolerated in a prison establishment.

Yet, life was tough in Reading, of course. One of the saddest events there was when Wilde has lost the custody of his children and his wife, Constance, came to the prison. She saw him there for the very last time, as she died just a short time later. One biographer described the situation: 'Mrs Wilde cast one long lingering glance inside and saw the convict-poet, who in deep mental distress… witnessed his degradation.'

Thomas Martin, in Stokes' view, a 'plant' put there by Haldane to give Wilde special treatment, was indeed guilty of breaking all the rules concerning prison officers and prisoners. He took Wilde drinks and biscuits every day – something that is technically a criminal offence called trafficking. On the exterior of every prison wall in Britain, next to the front gate, is a notice defining trafficking and giving the public dire warning of the consequences of giving prisoners anything without clearance. Martin later wrote an account of his life with Wilde in Reading. Wilde's fall from grace and respect is nowhere better illustrated than in Martin's memory of him having to turn away with all the other criminals when a 'star class' prisoner passed. That is, in modern terms, a first offender. Martin wrote: 'I have seen the poet having to stand with his face to the wall whilst a villainous looking ruffian passed by.' Martin was a quiet hero, in effect; on one occasion when Wilde was very ill, he went to fetch some beef tea for him, and he had to hide it, so the bottle of liquid was put under his coat. On the staircase on the way back, he was stopped and told to answer some questions by the chief warder. The hot beef tea spilled against his chest, burning him severely, yet he did not give in and admit what he was doing. He later recalled that 'The hot bottle burned against my breast like molten lead.'

Martin was later sacked for giving a biscuit to a child who had been imprisoned with the adults – normal practice at the time. Anthony Stokes is convinced that Martin was placed at Reading by Haldane, specifically to care for Oscar Wilde.

Wilde, as a sensitive and cultured man, was of course, living every day with the roughest elements in the criminal class. They suffered the usual prison regime of punishment and deprivation if they erred. Flogging was still used, and at one time Wilde heard a flogging in progress on a wing landing. He was so moved and appalled by this that he wrote to the papers. The *Daily Chronicle* printed his letter. Flogging was not abolished in England until 1939 and in Wilde's day the common criticism of such a tough punishment was perhaps best expressed by Mr Justice Keating in 1874, who replied to a questionnaire on the subject, saying:

> Does it deter others? I think not: a private flogging in a prison can scarcely have that effect; to be logical, the flogging should be as formerly, at the cart's tail: yet no one can doubt that the effect of such an exhibition would be to brutalise the masses… During more than 40 years of experience of criminal courts, I have observed crimes diminish under a steady and comparatively lenient administration of the law…

Wilde's protests had no effect. But his time in gaol was soon over after that; he was released from Reading on 18 May 1897. His last allowance of special privilege was that he could wear his own clothes as he walked out and that he was not in handcuffs. He then went to France and lived at Berneval-sur-Mer until his death in 1900. The *Times* carried a brief obituary and this summed up his tragic life as well as his rare genius:

> When he had served his sentence of two years' imprisonment, he was broken in health as well as bankrupt in fame and

fortune. Death has soon ended what must have been a life of wretchedness and unavailing regret.

They did add the words that he was 'a brilliant man of letters.'

It is thanks to the fact that Wilde had such notoriety that we know so much about prison life in the 1890s, from an authentic source of a man in a cell. The other spin-off benefits for literature and history have been that Wilde was arguably one of the most talented and gifted of all Victorian writers, and that talent was forced to express the deepest and most soul-searching words in his eventful life. In *De Profundis* we have a classic of prison literature and a work of rare spiritual exploration, all in one slim volume. He may have been a 'special prisoner' but that rare case gave us insider knowledge of prison life at its worst.

Oscar Wilde's reputation since these awful events has, of course, massively expanded and today he is still more influential than he was in his life, and in cultural areas even more than in drama, in many ways. He was, without doubt, one of the most troublesome and worrying prison inmates our prison system has ever had to cope with, but that sad episode in his short life added yet another dimension to the still resonant charisma and intellect of a unique artist and writer.

Wilde's father was almost a criminal, and in spite of his high reputation as a surgeon, he was part of a terribly embarrassing court case.

Admirers of the work of Oscar Wilde will always think of his trial, arrest and imprisonment in Reading Gaol as a central aspect of his life; it typifies his tendency to make enemies, to stir things up around him and to thrive on dissent and disagreement. The heart of his best work is a critique of many of the moral values of his time. But perhaps not so well known is the turbulent life of his father, Sir William Wilde, the famous Dublin doctor. The most sensational affair in his often scandalous life is one that involved a court case, and in many ways, the plaintiff was the person on trial.

William Wilde and his wife, Jane (who was a writer herself, known as 'Esperanza') were major figures in Dublin life and culture in the 1860s. He was a famous specialist in eye, nose and throat medicine and his knowledge and skills were widely admired. But he was also something of a womanizer, and in an atmosphere of what one biographer calls the 'Regency permissiveness' of the time, William Wilde acquired a reputation of a man who liked a good time and whose morals were not perhaps what they should have been.

Although Lady Wilde was clearly tolerant of her husband's small misdemeanours, when it came to a libel case against her, things became very difficult. It all began when a young woman called Mary Travers, who had been a patient of Sir William, began to spread rumours about her being raped by him while under chloroform. The incident had allegedly happened two years before this gossip appeared – and that is a strange fact in itself – and it seems more than accidental that she began to make trouble at the time when Wilde had been knighted in 1864 and when Lady Wilde was becoming a literary celebrity in Ireland.

Travers had been a patient of Wilde's since 1854, but was claiming that she had been 'ruined' in 1862; she wrote letters to newspapers with veiled allegations and even wrote a satire on the Wildes called 'Dr and Mrs Quilp.' But it was when Lady Wilde wrote a letter to Mary Travers' father that Mary took legal action. The letter was:

TOWER, BRAY May 6th

Sir, you may not be aware of the disreputable conduct of your daughter at Bray where she consorts with all the low newspaper boys of the place, employing them to disseminate offensive placards in which my name is given, and also tracts in which she makes it appear that she has had an intrigue with Sir William Wilde... I think it right to inform you, as no threat of additional insult shall ever extort money from our hands...

Mary Travers found out about this letter and sued Lady Wilde for libel; she took out a civil action, and had it been a criminal trial there would have been all kinds of unspeakable scrutiny and scandal, with Travers being very unlikely to have her man convicted, as there had been a gap of over two years since the alleged rape. In addition to that, the woman had acquired the reputation of being a fantasist and her statements were often laughably bizarre. But her counsel was Isaac Butt, a notable character around the city. That fact alone attracted a great deal of interest.

The story of the trial has been somewhat exaggerated in the pages of Frank Harris's book on Oscar Wilde, but at least Harris points out the strange nature of the events. The case was heard before Chief Justice Monahan in the Court of Common Pleas, and Mary Travers was claiming £2,000 damages for Lady Wilde's libel. Because Lady Wilde was married, her husband was part of the action, as a co-defendant for conformity.

In her writings and squibs on Wilde, Travers had written,

It is sad to think that in the nineteenth century a lady must not venture into a physician's study without being accompanied by a bodyguard to protect her.

She had published verses in local papers and written letters to *Saunders Newsletter*, so Wilde's defence had plenty of material there to use. But what emerged was a long and ambiguous relationship between Wilde and Travers, going back to his first treatment of her, when he cured her of a hearing problem.

Travers came to Wilde when she was just nineteen and partially deaf. He cured her and instead of the relationship ending there, a friendship developed. Wilde had written letters, given her gifts and even paid for a voyage to Australia for her. She had even been to dinner with the Wildes. There developed a voyeuristic interest in Travers' body: it was explained that she had a scar on her neck and that when treated by Wilde, she had to kneel down on a hassock before him. Wilde had also pared a painful corn she had. The narrative created by the defence was being compiled as one suggestive of a sensual and very tempting doctor-patient relationship.

When Mary Travers entered the witness box the court was treated to a graphic and detailed account of what Travers wanted to present as a seduction and as an act of an older man (and a professional) taking advantage of a simple young girl. Frank Harris summarises the tone and content very strongly:

> In October 1862, it appeared Lady Wilde was not at the house at Merrion Square but was away at Bray… Dr Wilde was alone in the house. Miss Travers called was admitted into Dr Wilde's study. He put her on her knees before him and bared her neck, pretending to examine the burn; he fondled her too much and pressed her to him… Somehow or other his hand got entangled in a chain at her neck… she declared that she lost consciousness.

The allegation was that Wilde had applied chloroform and then raped her while she was unconscious.

The judge asked Travers if she knew that she had been violated and she replied, 'Yes.' But there were complications and confusions; she had not been sure of the day when this was supposed to have happened, and she admitted that she had asked Wilde for money on several occasions. Of course, after the supposed assault, she kept on going back to Wilde's study. She even claimed that he had repeated the assault. The most damning event on her fabricated tale was when she was asked about the chloroform. She became confused and was not sure whether he had used a rag or a handkerchief, despite saying that she had seen him throw it into a fire. She could not even distinguish the smell of chloroform in court, and simply broke down.

Frank Harris commented on how Lady Wilde, when she had her turn in the box, was welcomed and applauded by the gallery, and he thought that even the judge and jury had been impressed by her. But Lady Wilde did not escape without some searching questions; she was asked if she hated Miss Travers and she replied that she did not hate anyone. Then the crucially important question was put – why did she not respond to the first letter she received from Travers telling her of her husband's conduct? She simply said that she had no interest in the matter.

Naturally, this whole affair could have had very serious consequences for William Wilde, and some writers have suggested that after the fiasco he was a broken man, but there is little to support this view. Chief Justice Monahan made the telling remark that had the trial been a criminal one, then no-one would have believed Miss Travers.

Isaac Butt was a smart character though, and he did well for Travers in a difficult situation. He made the point that the defence they had all witnessed was practically a justification of the libel. In the end, the whole point was whether or not there had been a nasty seduction, an exploitation of a vulnerable young woman in the hands of a respectable and well-liked medical man. Wilde never went into the witness box and that was seen by some as very strange. He was actually the defendant, even though the libel was principally directed at Mary Wilde.

In the end it was an ironical verdict. The jury retired for two hours and on their return they awarded Mary Travers damages of one farthing and noted that the sum should carry some costs. Frank Harris wrote in response:

> In other words they rated Miss Travers' virtue at the very lowest coin of the realm, while insisting that Sir William Wilde should pay a couple of thousands of pounds for having seduced her.

Wilde was supported by the prestigious journal of the British Medical Association, the *Lancet*. Just to reinforce how crazy Travers could be, after a journal in Ireland had written a piece in favour of Wilde in the affair, she took libel proceedings against them. Obviously she failed.

Yet such turbulent and juicy affairs tend to persist and also they circulate in the popular culture, and Richard Ellmann, the biographer of Oscar Wilde, has pointed out that Oscar would have heard this rhyme while he was at Trinity College:

> An eminent oculist lives in the Square,
> His skill is unrivalled, his talent is rare,

And if you will listen I'll certainly try
To tell how he opened Miss Travers's eye.

Nothing in this scandalous case affected his practice and reputation. His base in the city at Merrion Square has a plaque in his memory displayed to this day. In his own time, in 1873, the Royal Academy of Ireland gave him the Cunningham Gold Medal, its most important award.

16

THREE LITERARY ENTHUSIASTS

In complete contrast to all the other writers mentioned in this book, we have the category of those who could not resist a certain level of fascination with criminals and all things forensic and legal. The type tends to represent the kind of person who is in thrall of a gripping true crime story, and I have three outstanding examples, one from the Augustan age and one from Victoria's century. One was a journalist, one a jobbing writer, and the third an aristocrat with time on his hands. So it is to a certain extent the first may not be charged with any variety of rather twisted voyeurism, but the last of the three may indeed be so described.

The Augustan character in question was George Selwyn. His Victorian biographer noted that he was very strange in his hobbies: 'If human beings could be made pets… Selwyn would have fondled a hangman.' This aristocratic eccentric was born 11 August 1719 and he was at Eton at the same time as the future prime minister, Robert Walpole. Selwyn was the second son of Colonel John Selwyn, who had an estate in Matson, Gloucestershire. Selwyn Junior was supposedly given his wit and sense of rakish fun by his mother, Mary Faringdon, who was at court, and was one of the bedchamber women to Queen Caroline.

George was typical of his class in his Oxford days, incurring debts and learning bad habits. He was expelled by the dons for having a dinner at which he said the words, 'Drink this in remembrance of me' and was promptly in disgrace. What else was a young man to do at that point other than start a life of fun and gambling at the London clubs? He was drawn to Brooke's and White's clubs and there he wasted time spectacularly. One of the tales about White's was that when a man fell down dead at the door, he would be dragged inside so that patrons could lay wagers on the chances of his survival.

But Selwyn's true relish in life was to be in the proximity of criminals. One story of his life in this respect concerns his fun at seeing Lord Lovat executed after the Jacobite Rising of 1745:

> ...when rallied by some women for going to see the Jacobite Lovat's head cut off, he retorted sharply, 'I made full amends, for I went to see it sewn on again.' He had indeed done so, and given the company at the undertaker's a touch of his favourite blasphemy, for when the man of coffins had done his work and laid the body in the box, Selwyn, imitating the voice of the Lord Chancellor at the trial muttered, *You may rise...*

A story told of Selwyn in this context concerns Horace Walpole, the writer and collector:

> Horry Walpole had gone home one evening and was undressing when he heard a cry of 'Stop, thief!' He ran down the street and assisted the watch in catching a burglar in a neighbouring area. He had left George Selwyn at his cards in a club, and knowing the gentleman's taste for criminals, sent round a message. The coffee-house drawer stalked up to the club-room and said, 'Mr Walpole's compliments, and he has got a housebreaker for you.'

If we have to look for one of the most grotesque tales of Selwyn and his sick pastimes, it would be in his actions at the execution of Damiens, the man who tried to assassinate Louis XV. The would-be assassin was to die slowly and in great agony, torn by red-hot pincers and then fastened to horses whose movement would rip apart his body. George was there on the day and he forced himself through the crowd to be near the execution spot. The hangman knew him and called out, 'Make way for this gentlemen, he is an Englishman and a lover of my trade...'

Selwyn was supposedly fond of hanging around scaffolds, and would make sick jokes, as in the case of a criminal called Charles Fox. He was asked why he had not been to see this man hang, and Selwyn replied, 'I make a point of never going to rehearsals.' He died in 1791, and one biographer adds:

In his later days Selwyn still haunted the clubs, hanging about, sleepy, shrivelled, dilapidated in face and figure, yet still respected and dreaded by the youngsters, as 'the celebrated Mr Selwyn.'

In contrast, Robert Watson, born in 1848 in Manchester, although he had a similar fascination with criminals, explained this as part of his general curiosity about the world around him. He was known to the public as 'Diamond Bob' and was an authority on boxing. In Manchester as a boy, he could not avoid seeing the gaols. He looked with awe and fear at the Belle Vue Prison where Gissing was held, and at Salford Borough Prison. From his early days he was always aware of the crime stories around him; he was there, outside Salford Prison to watch when the Fenian 'Manchester Martyrs' who had killed a police sergeant were to be executed. He explains:

Their offence was in the death of Sergeant Brett, and it was in the deliverance of Burke and Casey from the prison van on its way to Belle Vue jail that the shot intended to break the lock… killed Brett.

He adds that the three men who were hanged lived within a few hundred yards of his birthplace and that he saw them at mass when they went to the same church.

Experiences such as that were at the root of his interests, and later on, as a writer in London, he became intrigued by the prisons and the criminal trials. On one occasion he arranged to visit the condemned cell at Newgate, and his writings give us one of the most powerful accounts of that place that exist in literature. He was conducted around the corridors and into the darkest places of the prison by William Scott, the Chief Warder, and the visit would have been around 1880, though Watson is never concerned about details of time and place in his narrative. Mr Scott gave Watson more than a tour: he gave him a taster of what aspects of prison life could be like.

At one point in the visit, Watson wrote about the time he spent in a small room with an interesting cupboard:

> It contained implements whereby prisoners are safely secured from escape and violence. I was handcuffed with various kinds of 'darbies' or 'bracelets' some of them allowing more scope than others, a special pair binding the hands tightly together, one on top of the other, and used on occasions when criminals are desperate... Mr Scott added, 'Criminals are not so violent as in Former years, indeed we seldom have reason to handcuff them. Men with small Wrists can sometimes extricate themselves, but I have never lost a prisoner.'

Watson, being curious to the point of excitement – largely of the kind we associate with the most ardent reader of the true crime genre, ends with the climax of the condemned cell. He reports closely on people who are involved in the execution ritual in prison work at that juncture:

> 'It is a very disagreeable duty to perform. Very.' With a shake of the head, a shrug of the shoulders and an expression as though they had swallowed a most unpleasant drug, they repeat, 'Very disagreeable. Very.'

Watson then explains what his readers would have most wanted to know. These same readers could have been enthralled by sketches of this same cell in the *Graphic* or the *Illustrated London News*, as these periodicals enjoyed depicting the worst scenes from Newgate and other gaols. He described the place lugubriously:

> Visitor and prisoner can only salute each other with a kiss, a last kiss, beyond that only conversation is possible...

Two warders, with the chief, accompany the person under sentence of death, and remain during the whole interview.

Linked to this is his account of the execution shed. Here he is precise, like a documentary-writer:

> From the condemned cell to the place of execution is not more than ten feet. The murderer is taken as quickly as possible across the floor to the prison door opposite. For the last time the light of day breaks upon him. The horrid bell hisses out the toll of death…

Watson, however, was far more than a voyeur or a crime reporter with a penchant for horror. He was interested in most aspects of the criminal law, describing lawyers and justices, police officers and witnesses. He also took time to explain the niceties of law in some notorious trials. Some of his discussions touch on the recently generated liaison between the press and the latest, more professional group of police detectives. The detective branch at Scotland Yard had been formed in 1842 and Watson was experiencing the work of the police and of the crime reporters around 1860. There was a certain aspect of novelty involved, particularly in one case, that of Walter Spriggs.

Spriggs was sentenced to penal servitude by Judge Graham, and the *Daily News* then called the judge 'the weakest judge of the English bench.' The police investigated the facts of a supposed alibi that the judge had called 'artistic.' Spriggs was found to be innocent and released. The newspaper took all the credit for this man's freedom, and there was a row, making everyone look to the police and their investigative methods, and more importantly, to the power of the press in such things, to influence the public. Watson understood completely, writing that he himself had looked into the case and his conclusion was as follows:

> The very root and branch, the fatal trap into which the whole business fell, was through the manner of identification.

The newspaper in question referred to this method... Here
was a grand opportunity for *The Evening News* worth far more
to the paper than the release of Mr Spriggs...

Watson actually found out the modus operandi of the detective
involved and also errors and omissions.

Watson's bestseller was his book *Louise Reignier* (1895), subtitled,
'The Communion of Crime and Criminals: A True Story.' This was
his only crime novel and was set in both London and Paris. The work
for the novel included research undertaken on a trip to Wormwood
Scrubs, and he explains this in his memoirs:

> It was for the purpose of writing prison scenes in *Louise
> Reignier* that special permission was given me by the Home
> Office on two occasions to inspect Wormwood Scrubs,
> accompanied by Mr Justus Hill, who made three sketches for
> the novel, depicting prisoners and their general behaviour. No
> restriction was placed upon the order from the Home Office,
> privileges being accorded such as seldom falls to the lot of
> visitors, no matter how distinguished.

His conclusion about being inside a prison was that 'after a few hours
incarceration' he reflected and he felt trepidation:

> The death-like stillness, recollection of desperate criminals,
> together with the terrible crimes recalled by my presence in
> the cells they once occupied, rendered me a trifle uncertain as
> to what might occur.

One further stage of his involvement with criminals, however,
is that one of that class was in fact his friend. This was Frank
Tarbeaux, one of the men in the so-called 'Cutlass Case.' This was
tried at the Old Bailey on 17 June 1895. Tarbeaux was in the
dock, charged with breaking the peace and wounding; he had
assaulted a man called Arthur Cockburn after a night out at a

club in Regent Street. Tarbeaux, Cockburn, Carroll Woodward (a friend of Tarbeaux's) and a bookmaker called Savile had enjoyed drinks until early in the morning, and then there was a fight. Savile testified that he saw Tarbeaux and Woodward attack Cockburn, and then they turned on him. Cockburn explained in court what happened to him:

> The prisoner struck me on the left cheek... I fell off the chair... I could not say whether it was a blow with a fist or with some instrument... he kicked me when I was on the ground, I felt something, and my jaw was broken.

There was a long-standing grudge relating to a card-game played between them in Margate and this appears to have been a drunken revenge. A constable was called and arrests were made. The argument from Tarbeaux was that he had been drinking heavily and had struck out in self-defence. The wounds on Cockburn included an incised wound on the cheek, made by a blade, so the case became known as the 'Cutlass Case' because the surgeon saw these weapons and felt that one had been used on Cockburn.

Tarbeaux had earlier been given bail and had gone over to France during his bail period. Watson explains this by writing that they were 'anxious to see some friends abroad' but they were too late for the first trial at the old Bailey. The result was, as Watson puts it, 'Finally, Tarbeaux answered the call of justice and paid the penalty.' He was sentenced to three years of penal servitude. There was definitely something wild in the man. Watson and Tarbeaux were friends, and the wild gambler called Watson 'Bobby.' The writer clearly admired his friend a great deal, saying that he was sometimes 'awe-inspiring' in conversation. But the wild side was there. Watson tells a tale of cruelty in this respect, recalling that once they were walking and saw a cat. Watson then took out a stiletto knife and 'shot it in the air swift as an assegai, and caught the cat in the rear of its anatomy.'

Such was Robert Watson, writer, investigative journalist and crime aficionado. His memoirs educated readers of the 1890s with a wide range of topics related to the criminal justice system, and it is clear from his account of his formative years in Manchester that his ability in these matters was down to the prevalence of crime in his native streets and to the gloomy gaols that occupied his daily horizon. He summed up his connection with crime with these simple words in his autobiography: 'Criminal courts and prison life have occupied my attention since a boy, and perforce, be inseparable from this history.'

My third documentary 'jobbing' writer is one who deserves to be much more widely known and read. He is perhaps defined as a provincial writer, but he made a career in London and was published by some major publishers late in his life.

It is in Bradford, perhaps, more than in any other Yorkshire Victorian city, that the literary culture around the new aspirations to read and write both high quality literature and popular narratives, is apparent. There are many reasons for this: the influx of German immigrants who brought their love of higher cultural pursuits, the appeal of a bohemian, cosmopolitan culture to the new middle class; and, most of all, to the energy of individuals. In Bradford there was a 'nest of singing birds' (as Dr Johnson described his literary coterie) gathered around various clubs, coffee houses and societies, and a key figure in this was the writer and journalist, James Burnley.

The time was right for such a figure to emerge. The local civic pride was developing in step with the legislation for incorporation (Bradford being made a County Borough in 1889) and with the establishment of literary and philosophical societies such as those thriving in Leeds and Hull in the mid-Victorian years. As Asa Briggs puts it when comparing Leeds and Bradford: 'Bradford was the first of the two communities to sponsor a handsome new public building which was designed to "elevate" taste and meet the cultural needs of a business metropolis' and also, with St George's Hall, Briggs points out, 'What happened inside it was to raise the tone of society also.'

A fundamental part of this Bradford culture, though, was in the people, not simply in the buildings and grand public gestures of politicians. Writing was becoming a booming local cultural product, offering outlets for the mediocre enthusiast as well as the genuine creative spirit. James Burnley was at the heart of this, as editor, poet, comedian and serious social commentator. As Ian Dewhirst has pointed out, the authors being published could range from clergymen to anonymous operatives from the factory floor. Burnley came on the literary scene with a few poems and a knowledge of the London theatre in the 1860s, and soon became involved with the group of writers around the *Bradford Observer* and the *Bradford Review*.

Several writers of later years have commented on the cultural richness and diversity of late Victorian Bradford, so it is not difficult to imagine the context in which Burley thrived. W. Riley, for instance, in his autobiography, notes:

> Good reference libraries were close at hand; good lectures were available; cultured men and women were ready to stimulate and encourage the serious student. As I recall to mind the opportunities that then presented themselves I appropriate to myself the well-known line of Wordsworth 'Bliss was it in that dawn to be alive.'

Peter Holdsworth has pointed out the importance of this setting for the young J. B. Pristley, commenting that '… in his youth Bradford was… culturally dynamic. Theatre, literary pursuits, sport and the visual arts thrived alongside a host of societies.'

But in the earlier period, when Burnley arrived, there was a notable difference to the more institutionalized developments of the fin de siècle Bradford. The writing was more directly comprehensive, aware of what working men wanted in their reading, as well as supplying reading matter for the middle class. Burnley had such a wide range of writing ability that he could fit in with the drinkers and workers at Thomas Nicholson's eating house in Kirkgate, talking to almanac writers and singers, but also dining with the large-scale entrepreneurs whose lives he was to write about in his best-selling book, *The Romance of Modern Industry* (1886).

Burnley was born in Shipley in 1842 and began his long publishing career with a volume of poems, *Idonia and Other Poems* (1869).

His talents extended to other compositions such as plays, sketches, travel writing, fiction and journalism. He became most celebrated as 'The Saunterer,' the man who produced the almanac, *The Saunterer's Satchel* throughout the last decades of the century, and also well known for his 'sketch books' – *Phases of Bradford Life* (1871) and *West Riding Sketches* (1875). These two books illustrate the special qualities that made Burnley central to this Bradford literary culture; his mix of serious commentary and accessible humour, along with his ability to embrace the range of cultural references from folklore to modern industrial processes. In fact, his most successful books celebrated the woollen industry and the wider Victorian preoccupations with 'rags to riches' themes in the age of Samuel Smiles and his phenomenal best-seller, *Self-Help* (1859). His book, *The History of Wool and Wool-Combing* (1889) appears to have made his name national and provide him with access to the drawing-rooms of the wealthy.

What defines Burnley's importance to Bradford writing and to the massive success of the whole group of journalists and poets around him are his local publishing achievements, largely with the founding of the *Yorkshireman* in 1875 which begun as a monthly. In later years, as one memoirist puts it, 'he resided in London; and made a host of friends among the leading literati of the metropolis.' In other words, here we have a writer who was one of a class who succeeded in the wake of the huge ocean liner that was dominating the age – the shrine of 'literature' – and Burnley was a 'bookman' in that context, one of the smaller vessels perhaps, to follow the metaphor.

But for the student of crime writing, his importance is illustrated when we look closer at the nature of the almanac, *The Saunterer's Satchel*. Here was a publication that stands out in its time. The almanac, as established in the working-class author tradition, notably in Barnsley, Halifax and Leeds, had been primarily a calendar with anniversaries and local adverts (notably of patent medicines) and perhaps the first type of popular publication supplying local dialect verse and narrative that provided sustenance for the local and civic pride so evident at the time. The most celebrated almanac, John Hartley's *Clock Almanac*, exemplifies this. An average issue would contain humorous pieces, anecdotes and rhymes, all very much to the popular taste and similar to the material in demand for penny readings and for dialect recitals such as those given by Ben Preston, following afternoon tea and Bible classes. Naturally, writing about the new urban life, there were accounts of transgressions. The possibilities of breaking the law were everywhere present.

The success of penny readings was obviously a factor. London publishers were producing hardback volumes for these readings by the 1870s, notably Frederick Warne. Stories of wanderings from the straight and narrow figured there. But also, Burnley enjoyed the life of that kind of writer who goes down into the lives of the masses, criminal or otherwise, and reports on the experience to his middle class readers.

In his book, *Phases of Bradford Life*, in which Burnley collected many of his local writings, he has a piece on 'Coffee House Life' and this makes clear exactly what it was like to be involved in this 'mind communion:'

> Here in Bradford there still exist coffee rooms where discussion on the topics of the day constitute a special feature, and where almost any night may be heard debates equal in vigour, if not in ability, to any heard within the walls of the House of Commons.

He writes of 'Straycock's temperance Hotel' in a dingy court off Kirkgate, and has gentle fun at the expense of a crowd of regulars. Even more pastiche and satire are injected into a sketch called 'Barnacle's Evening Party,' in which Dickens' Pickwick Club is echoed. The guest list is an exaggeration of the range of writers who perhaps really did gather in the Bradford writers' circles of the age. They include such worthies as 'Abimelech Flavonius de Smithkins, the great local author and historian of Wibsey Slack' and 'Mr Silvanio, the tragedian.' Barnacles provides his guests with a selection of literature for the party, and this includes, 'Long yarns by an Old Spinner – a most amusing volume' and 'Looming in the distance – a three-volume novel by the author of *Fell'd at Last*.'

There were some remarkable characters in the circle around Burnley and their enthusiasm and high level of literary appreciation is typified by J. Arthur Binns, whom Burnley describes in this way:

> He was... A man of some leisure and disclosed to me a mind better stored with literary knowledge than that of any man I have ever known... He was chairman of the library committee of the old Mechanics' Institute. He knew the poets so thoroughly that he had many of their best pieces literally off by heart. He could recite the whole of Pope's Essay on Man and reel off poems and stanzas by Shelley...

To Bradford generally, Binns was known as the President of the Third Equitable Building Society.

Burnley was always hankering after a bohemian literary life and a Yorkshire Literary Union was formed in April 1870. Burnley recalled,

> It must not be imagined that the Bradford writers did not chum together socially as well as in literary matters... There was a strain of Bohemianism about some of us...

He clearly hankered for a mix of café society and serious literary production, and his works reflect this diversity.

Burnley's work in Bradford has a greater significance than has been given to him. As a writer, propagandist for social progress and the amelioration of man through work and cultural fulfilment, Burnley surely deserves to be re-read. His writings provide valuable evidence of important social and cultural history; but far more important than this is his place in the chronicles of both an emerging working-class interest in literature and in the middle-class acquisition of their own cultural values in the acceptance of civic pride and local belonging. All this came at a time when English literature was only just in the process of becoming recognized as a subject with meaning and status. But it was the Bradford setting, and its unique contributions to the new publishing enterprises that gave Burnley his real break as a writer. As he puts it in the introduction to *West Riding Sketches*:

> In the West Riding… the old and new clash together so indiscriminately, the prose and the poetry intermingle so curiously, that it requires one to be native and to the manor born to distinguish the lines of demarcation.

Burnley was very much the creation of that growth of regional consciousness born of civic pride, and the writers in his circle certainly understood that Yorkshire was an entity, as part of a concept of 'The North,' that it was also a state of mind that needed a literature of its own, largely to counteract the stereotypes given to places north of the Trent by London writers.

In matters of crime and law, Burnley could not resist visiting a prison, just as he had visited every other type of institution in his life as a local journalist, and in the 1870s he went to one of the oldest and most infamous prisons in the land – Wakefield. Even today, it is still a name equated with the housing and containment of some of the most notoriously troublesome and recalcitrant prisoners we have incarcerated. In his time, the phrase 'sent to Wakefield' was in common use meaning 'gone to prison' such was the image of the Wakefield House of Correction as it was known then in the public consciousness. His title for the account of the visit is 'Sent to Wakefield' and he wrote in that work:

> People living outside the limits of the West Riding have no idea of the dreadful import of the three words which I have placed at the head of this sketch.

Like Watson, he toured the place with a guide – a policeman called Robert. We then have a full documentary narrative of the day's sights, beginning with his being scrutinized, and then he provides some statistics:

> The total number of prisoners in the House that June morning was 1291, made up as follows – 1010 males, 235 females and

46 military prisoners. The average daily admittance was 26 people; for the year 1873 the total number of admittances was 8379 prisoners.

He then gives a powerful account of the material world of the interior:

> We pass hundreds of massive wooden doors, on the inner side of which… there are as many prisoners, constituting collectively such an army of desperadoes, such a concentration of brutality and viciousness, of depravity and worthlessness, as, if let loose, would be sufficient to speedily overpower all of the hundred and sixty officials who are engaged keeping watch over them.

Finally, Burnley manages to speak to an inmate, and asks if the man sleeps. The man answers that he sometimes does, and Burnley reflects, 'What a horrid thought it was to fancy oneself sleeping there, alone, in the dead of night, in the darkness!' Other encounters include the views of the workrooms and the exercise yard, and the treadmill. His description is one of the best we have from the period of their use (from c. 1820–1890 in most cases):

> A small engine is kept running with the wheels, as a sort of steadying power, but round and round the wheels go with a terribly persistent monotony. This work is given as punishment for breaking regulations and it is so hard that only those men whom the doctor certifies as of first-class physical capabilities can be put to it. A grim warder stands over them, watching every step they take. The front of the wheel is boxed off into compartments, each admitting one treader at a time, so that not only is a man unable to speak to, but he unable to see any of his fellows…

When he finally leaves the place he reflects on how impressed he was with the running of the 'monster prison-house.' His trope for the whole experience was the use of Dante entering Hell with his poet-guide, Virgil. Simple though that image is, it provides the most informative way of explaining the attitude of the writers and poets who ventured into the prisons of Britain at the time of one of the quietest revolutions we have had in social history – the nationalisation of prisons and the gradual abandonment of many provincial gaols which had been known to the great reformer John Howard, back in the 1770s.

Visiting prisons and joining the crowds at executions was a common pastime for many, from different walks of life. In his memoirs, Colonel Frederick Wellesley, the grand-nephew of the Duke of Wellington, explains various ways of obtaining seats or access to rooms from where to watch hangings. He was present at several of these, and for the hanging of Muller, the first 'railway murderer' he paid a guinea to enter an upstairs room in a public house from where he could watch the execution. He relished a criminal anecdote, and at one time, after visiting Newgate himself, he took a friend, writing about it as if it was a pleasant recreation:

> On another occasion when I took a foreigner to see the prison we were taken round by the senior warder… We saw in one of the cells a man who had been condemned to death for setting fire to a house which he had previously insured, thereby causing the death by burning of one of the inmates. His sentence had just been commuted and he was picking oakum.

These three provide examples of writers who were fascinated by crime in general, and, in Selwyn's case, by punishment as well. When it came to executions, which were public until 1868, several writers were drawn to join the noisy throng on scaffold day. When the killer of Lord Russell, his servant Courvoisier, was hanged in 1840, among the crowd of 40,000 were the novelists Thackeray and Dickens, and one report added that 'six hundred persons of distinction' were there. Dickens was always curious about crime and criminals, but after that awful sight, he wrote: 'I came away from Snow Hill that morning

with a disgust for murder, but it was for the murder I saw done…
I feel myself ashamed and degraded.'

However, it is not difficult to see why so many writers have had
both the curiosity and the revulsion that Dickens expressed. Thomas
Hardy was in the habit of watching through binoculars on hanging
days, and, as a teenager, had witnessed the hanging of murderess
Martha Browne in August 1856. He later noted,

> what a fine figure she showed against the sky as she hung in
> the misty rain and how the tight black silk gown set off her
> shape as she wheeled half round and back…

This was the inspiration for the hanging of Tess in *Tess of the
D'Urbervilles*, so we have a classic instance of the effect on the writer's
imagination of a specific criminal.

Such correlations between criminals and writers are easy to
locate, but actual fascination and close scrutiny of criminals, or even
friendship with them, are not so common. In this respect, of all the
voyeurs, George Selwyn stands out as a special case – perhaps as one
of a 'sick' mind. But there is no doubt that from earliest times to
1868, public hangings were on par with circuses and freak shows; the
public enjoyed a good hanging as much as staring at The Elephant
Man or The Bearded Lady. Such was the fascination with crime
that writers had to be informed and try to understand the nature of
the appeal of such morbid interest. His writing was no more than
what would be expected of dilettanti but his perverted interests do
mirror the kind of scrutiny and fascination with execution which
absorbed so many creative writers in the eighteenth and nineteenth
centuries.

SOME CONCLUSIONS

In the Georgian and Victorian years, creative writers were perhaps not as well acquainted with the insides of prisons as the journalists, editors and pamphleteers; it is clear from my subjects that writers guilty of crimes other than political ones are few and far between.

Nevertheless, there are many instances of writers being involved in the prison system for a range of crimes, and I have had to choose carefully when it came to selecting the writers to include. For instance, the case of W. T. Stead is one of the most outstanding cases, but I have thought of him as a journalist with an important point to make in his 'undercover' act of buying a teenage girl from her mother for £5 in order to highlight the ease with which crooks could obtain girls for prostitution. Stead was the editor of the *Pall Mall Gazette* and he published a series of articles on the subject headed 'The Maiden Tribute of Modern Babylon.' He was sentenced to three months in prison.

Another related area of interest is in the topic of writers who took a special interest in prison life. Even if we leave out the documentarists such as Mayhew and Binny, we are left with a number of minor, lesser-known writers, often provincial, a typical example being James Burnley, who has left one of the best accounts of prison life from the period that we have. When Burnley arrived on the literary scene in Bradford (before moving to London and mixing with the likes of Dickens), there was a notable difference to the more institutionalized developments of the fin de siecle Bradford. The writing was more directly comprehensive, aware of what working men wanted in their reading, as well as supplying reading matter for the middle classes.

Other writers on the fringe of being subjects here include the police court missionaries. These were the Christian volunteers who did probation work before there was a probation service (which arrived in 1907). In the last decades of Victorian Britain, the results of the Industrial Revolution and massive urban growth, together with huge scale immigration into London from Eastern Europe and Russia, meant that 'everyday' minor crime spread wider and went deeper: that is to say, as well as creating problems in the courts, this also added to penal issues such as the uncertainties about the prison system. In 1877 the prisons had been effectively nationalised and regimented, being run by military men. In terms of the efforts to provide help with rehabilitation, the emphasis was still on silence, reflection and hard work. Of course, until the end of the century, most local prisons had a full mix of ages, gender, and populations nurturing what was called 'contamination' – the first offenders being corrupted by old lags. Until the early Edwardian years, many gaols still had women offenders inside giving birth to children.

This wider view gives us an insight into exactly how important the Police Court Missionaries were in that social context. They reclaimed a large number of people who, without them, would have slipped into habitual crime as their only option, living in the sad and desperate underclass. The writings of these men are, again, on the fringe – almost within my scope – and they deserve a mention.

There is no shortage of such material by writers who were fascinated by prisons in these two hundred years, yet when it came to finding writers who really knew prison cells or who had connections with those who did so, the written records are of a very special quality. This is perhaps exemplified best by William Cooper's dramatic memoirs and by Oscar Wilde's masterpiece, *De Profundis*.

More general conclusions have to address the fact that although the image of the Georgian and Victorian prisons is one of horrendous and formidable experience of oblivion, a chamber next door to hell, there is an argument for insisting that for some, as I have shown, prison life was actually conducive to creative work. *Little Dorrit* is arguably the one creative work with prison at its heart which stands out as being embedded in the criminal connection of the author. As one writer noted in his analysis of prison literature in reference to Dickens,

> …Dickens created a prison novel unsurpassable in its panoramic intensity – if only because social panoramas in the manner of Dickens, Thackeray or Honore de Balzac are no longer present in the novelist's imagination. After *Little Dorrit*, what else was to be done?

We generally expect transformations, if not staggering epiphanies, from creative souls trapped and captured behind bars; if the criminal experience happens to be happening to a friend or relative, we perhaps still assume that there will be an impact on the writer. Yet in fact, in most cases the incarceration is not necessarily so, and the criminal act (or even alleged criminal act) is often erased or skipped over in autobiographical reflection. Certainly this was the case with Jane Austen who pretended her aunt's forensic difficulties never really existed. In contrast, such biography may offer the worst possible imaginable crushing of the spirit, as no doubt was the case with Oscar Wilde.

It would be a simple conclusion to say that most writers' crimes are defined as 'political' – related to their intellectual beliefs. Yet social history throws up quite a variety, if we cast the net back further than c. 1700. Before that, there are plenty of cases in which writers have had to act criminally through desperate poverty, and there have also been plenty of writers who were ruffians. Ben Jonson killed a fellow actor in a duel in 1598, pleaded benefit of clergy by reciting the neck verse, and was acquitted, although he was branded a felon. Since medieval times, a man in the dock facing a murder charge could have a chance of avoiding death by claiming that he was a clergyman and could recite the 'neck verse' (usually in Latin but later not necessarily so) which was Psalm 51, verse 1:

> Have mercy upon me oh God, according to thy loving kindness: according unto the multitude of thy tender mercies blot out my transgressions.

This was abolished in 1827 by the Criminal Justice Act; before this, all felonies were capital offences unless benefit of clergy was a factor. A felony was any offence which resulted in the person forfeiting all land and goods to the Crown and being sentenced to death.

Yet on the whole, the writers who figure most prominently in this context are those who tried to live beyond their means or who tended to go too far with their opinions in print. The one outstanding example of a writer who has come to represent both the transgression of a criminal code on par with 'common criminals' while at the same time representing something much more significant is Oscar Wilde. As Matthew Sweet said in this respect, discussing the fact that when Wilde was arrested at the Cadogan Hotel on 5 April 1895, he was assumed to have the *Yellow Book* under his arm, whereas he simply had a novel:

> The assumption was that this was *The Yellow Book*, the journal of Aesthetic art and literature with which Beardsley was strongly identified. Sufficient numbers of people made that assumption for a sizeable crowd to assemble outside the Vigo Street offices of its publishers, the Bodley Head, and pelt the windows with stones…

Some few writers saw criminals from the magistrate's bench. H. Rider Haggard, for instance, though he was far more interested in Zulu culture and history, did write incisively about the offenders he met while on the bench in his Norfolk parish. In the 1890s, he cheerfully compared the past and present situation with regard to the criminals who had stood before him:

> I am glad to say that they [crime statistics] show a marked and progressive diminution, owing chiefly, I believe, to the spread of education among the classes from which spring the majority of criminals.

There is also a very straightforward way to see the fascination with crime in the lives of so many writers: it relates to the old adage that a writer can't write an experience until he or she has lived it. This is an extension of simple, dogged research, just as a historical novelist might walk a battlefield or a royal court; yet there is an extra dimension here, and arguably it relates to that need writers have to accept the challenge of empathy – to write empathically to such an extent that they are 'inside the skin' of the characters they create. Moreover, a prison or a courtroom tends to provide a location which is already charged with the vestiges of human drama. A perusal of any record from a court of criminal appeal in the days of hanging will confirm this view of the writer and the world of social transgression.

An interesting perspective on the kind of literary interests reflected in my essays is the parallel growth of popular true crime books and magazines. Although many of the writers I have discussed did of course write about crime and law, their interest was not necessarily of a kind that would explore the possibilities offered by popular narrative, although Conan Doyle does exemplify that development. In fact, as 'true crime' was slowly established in the cheap magazines, the 'penny dreadfuls' of the Victorian period, the more literary, highbrow use of crime in themes and materials for narrative, and such genres as documentary and biography, came through with their own readership. At the basis of this there was also a concomitant interest in the criminal law and the ritualistic drama of the courts. In the 1890s and in the early years of the twentieth century, there were developments in the law and in the criminal justice system which had a massive impact on writers, because there was human drama built into these matters. Most significant in this respect is surely the establishment of the court of criminal appeal in 1907: an institution that lends itself to the highest, most tense drama conceivable. A man would stand in the dock, facing his 'last chance' hearing, with one door leading to freedom or at least a prison sentence, and the other door to the scaffold.

It would not be difficult to argue that the presiding genius over my theme would be that of Thomas de Quincey. In his rambling pastiche, the dark comedic essay *On Murder Considered as One of the Fine Arts*, he anticipated my major theme: the fascination of matters criminal to the writer. He saw that transgression is endlessly intriguing and has always been there in the centre of literary and artistic interest. In taking up the contemporary topic of the Ratcliffe Highway murders (1811) he was hinting that supposed everyday trivia – the daily occurrence of violent crime and homicide – could surprisingly provide food for thought, and indeed for intellectual types as well as for the men who loved to chat about the news in the crowded coffee houses. I have admittedly taken my cue from his following assertion (tongue in cheek of course):

> I am for morality and always shall be, and for virtue and all that; and I do affirm... that murder is an improper line of conduct... and that any man who deals in murder must have very improper ways of dealing... but what then? Everything in this world has two handles. Murder, may be laid upon by its moral handles... or it may also be treated aesthetically as the Germans call it – that is, in relation to good taste.

His gentle and clever spoof essay was out to invite his readers to consider more deeply why they had a fascination with criminal connections.

In that silliness, in his wonderfully rich take on the human curiosity about transgression, we have the germ of the more popular interest in criminals – the kind of thing we have for instance in the popular ephemera in which we have descriptions such as these from a publisher's catalogue:

> **Biographical Sketch of Alexander Millar**, who was executed at Stirling on the 8th April, 1837, for the murder of William Jarvie, near Dennyloadhead. Communicated by the prisoner after his condemnation to which is added a brief narrative of his trial and a particular account of his behaviour...
>
> Or,
>
> **The Bloody Register**. A select and judicious collection of the most remarkable trials for murder, treason, rape, sodomy,

highway robbery, piracy, house breaking, perjury, forgery and other high crimes and misdemeanours from the year 1700 to the year 1764 inclusive.

De Quincey understood that the public were beginning to want more than a mere account of the more bloodthirsty elements in 'horrible crime' and that the study of criminal behaviour could lead to a deeper understanding of human motivation and deviance. Of course, this had always been there, principally in the drama; Shakespeare's plays are rich in the depiction of transgression and its profiles of human emotions, from guilt to hatred and from illicit desire to cruelty and abuse. But in the newer genres of fiction and discursive prose there was a new position for such texts to occupy, and that was not necessarily in the ephemera.

From the years of the birth of the novel, with Defoe, we have the usual dual traditions of popular and highbrow, yet from the beginning, crime and criminals had occupied a place in bright focus – the upper classes and the progressive middle classes who could buy or borrow the new books not only had a fascination with the results of crime, but, as we have seen with Jane Austen's aunt, prison could beckon for them also.

Most of my essays feature a society made on fragile ice rather than on solid foundations; the criminal justice system and the mechanisms of debt and credit made the possibility of sudden ruin and oblivion something open to anyone. After all, the records of state trials are packed with tales of the rich and powerful, people who had taken one step too far into forbidden ground or who had made one terrible mistake. As the Georgian society opened up its vast empire, and trade became something ventured into for huge profit and risk, so the perils of such enterprise proliferated, and a man could be rich and wanted one day, and then impoverished and reviled the next. Until the reforms of the mid-Victorian times, society had so many offences on the statutes, and so many social dangers, that oblivion existed in the street next to prosperity.

An important change with regard to debt and its punishment was the arrival of the County Courts and the notion of small claims in the legal system, with the County Courts Act of 1846. But debtors still were driven to extremes, many running away and living overseas.

The Victorian age saw such extremes of wealth and poverty, as the Industrial Revolution accelerated, that any social class which could not generate wealth enough to survive, (with nothing to save the unfortunate but the workhouses) would go to the wall. Writers and journalists trying to exist as freelancers in that milieu would struggle. Not every writer found himself welcome at the society dinners that authors' clubs held in London; many lived in poverty, and the prison was sometimes their destiny. Only when, by the 1890s, the business of writing was made more professional by the creation of proper agencies and copyright laws, was there a little more security for the writers who existed at the lean end of the spectrum, quite the opposite of the bestseller writers.

A fitting ending to this survey is to return to the question of the crimes themselves. All but one or two of the offences discussed above were hardly dangerous transgressions. In truth, they were offences committed at times when there were other morals and beliefs. It is tempting to end with a point about the reversals of this, as when the state effects an unspeakable act against the writer, even outside the prison walls, perhaps typified in Russia by the Tsar's treatment of Dostoievski and other Decembrists when he blindfolded them, believing they were to be shot, and then removed the cloth and sent them to Siberia. There is a metaphor there for the plight of the writer at the mercy of those who fear free thinking and free expression. In fact, the Regency during this period does not seem so far away from the Tsar in some respects, and this is seen in the treatment of writers and other artists.

ACKNOWLEDGEMENTS

Thanks go to other writers and historians who have helped with suggestions and ideas when planning this book. Research would have been impossible without help from staff at Lincolnshire Archives and at the University of Hull. For help with sources for Robert Peddie, thanks go to staff at the East Riding Archives in Beverley. Similarly, for material on the Chartist prisoners at Northallerton, thanks go to the staff there who helped in the compilation of my history of that prison, *House of Care* (Bar None Books, 2009).

As usual in these works of interdisciplinary interest, much thought came from conversations with other writers, and, of course, material from some recent works on this period proved very useful indeed. Scholarship in the last decade has put a close focus on the later Victorian years and writers have proved to be essential sources in this work.

BIBLIOGRAPHY AND SOURCES

In the Georgian and Victorian years, writers and prison sentences were almost always related to some species of sedition, libel or debt. Fortunately for historians of such experience, writers themselves generally could not resist writing prison memoirs, and, with the expansion of the true crime genre and the growth of interest in crime history, sources for such enquiries are not rare. However, many of them are obscure, so the search has been long though enjoyable. The sources here represent a mix of memoirs, archives and writings in what may be called ephemera. Often the ephemera present the most useful and interesting sources, many of which tend to come from personal witness and documentary insight, at a time when the genre of documentary was burgeoning – the middle years of Victoria's reign.

One of the real pleasures of gathering material for these stories has been the collation and comparison involved in relating autobiography to the facts gathered by the writers in the great period of social documentary in Britain between 1850 and 1890, when prison and police court life became the subject of intense interest, and as the criminal justice system experienced radical change.

As the market for lawyers' memoirs also grew, notably from the middle years of the nineteenth century, so the possibilities for legal and criminal subjects to be considered as suitable topics of interest for literary men expanded, and so very useful sources are in rather obscure autobiographical texts. The criminal interests of rather obscure writers and editors are to be found in the accounts of their court cases, and lawyers who dabbled with the pen tended to recall such cases. Without these footnotes of history, access to the minutiae of prison experience would be much harder to achieve.

Primary Sources
Note: Dates of first publication are given in brackets before details of the text cited.

Books

Anonymous. *A narrative of the cruelties & abuses acted by Isaac Dennis, keeper, his wife and servants, in the prison of Newgate, in the city of Bristol, upon the people of the Lord in scorn called Quakers.* (Bristol, 1683)
———· *The Newgate Calendar.* (Publisher unknown, c. 1880s)
———· *Old Bailey Experience.* (James Fraser, 1833)
Austen-Leigh, J. E. *A Memoir of Jane Austen* (1870). (Oxford University Press, 2008)
Barrett, Andrew and Christopher Harrison. *Crime and Punishment in England: A Sourcebook* (University College London Press, 1999)
Boswell, James. *Journals 1761–1795.* Edited by John Wain. (Heinemann, 1991)
———· *Boswell's London Journal 1762–1763.* Edited by Frederick A Pottle. (Penguin, 1966)
———· *The Life of Samuel Johnson* (1791). (The Times Book Club, 1912)
Burnley, James. *West Riding Sketches.* (Hodder and Stoughton, 1875)
Caminada, Jerome. *Caminada the Crime Buster* (1895). First published as *Twenty-Five Years of Detective Life* (John Heywood, 1895). (True Crime Library, 1996)
Cobbett, William. *Rural Rides* (1830). (Penguin, 1967)
———· *Remarks on Sir F Burdett's letter to his Constituents on the Power of Imprisonment by the House of Commons.* (T. Brook, 1810)
Collins, L. C. *Life and Memoirs of John Churton Collins.* (Bodley Head, 1907)
Combe, William. *Dr Syntax: His Three Tours.* (Frederick Warne, 1858)
Cooper, Thomas. *The Life of Thomas Cooper.* (Hodder and Stoughton, 1872)
Davitt, Michael. *Leaves from a Prison Diary* (1885). (Irish University Press, 1972)
Dickens, Charles. *Sketches by Boz* (1836). (Hazell, Watson and Viney, 1935)
Greville, Charles. *The Diaries.* Edited by Edward Pearce. (Pimlico, 2006)
Griffiths, Arthur. *Secrets of the Prison-House.* (Chapman and Hall, 1894)
Haggard, H Rider. *A Farmer's Year* (1899). (Cresset, 1987)
Hawkins, Henry. *Reminiscences.* (Nelson, 1910)
Howard, John. *The State of the Prisons* (1777). (J. M. Dent, 1960)
Hunt, Leigh. *The Literary Examiner.* (Hunt, 1823)
———· *Autobiography.* (Smith, Elder, 1860)

_____· *Correspondence.* (Smith, Elder, 1862)

Johnson, Samuel. 'Richard Savage' in *Lives of the Poets* (1779–1781). (Oxford University Press, 1973)

_____· *Idler* (1759). (C. Cooke, 1818)

Keats, John. *Selected Letters.* (Oxford University Press, 1970)

Mayhew, Henry and John Binny. *The Criminal Prisons of London.* (Griffin, Bohn and Co., 1862)

Milne, James. *Memoirs of a Bookman.* (John Murray, 1934)

Mitchel, John. *Jail Journal* (1913). (Sphere, 1983)

Peddie, Robert. *The Dungeon Harp.* (Author, 1844)

Savage, Richard. *An Author to be Lett* (1729). Edited by James Sutherland. Augustan Reprint Society edition. (William Andrews Clark Memorial Library, 1960)

Southey, Robert. *Letters from England* (1807). (Sutton, 1984)

Tristan, Flora. *The London Journal of Flora Tristan* (1842). (Virago, 1982)

Tuke, Samuel. *Description of the Retreat* (1813). (Process Press, 1984)

Watson, Robert Patrick. *Memoirs.* (Smith Ainslie, 1899)

Wellesley, Col. Frederick. *Recollections of a Soldier-Diplomat.* (Hutchinson, 1947)

Wilde, Oscar. *The Ballad of Reading Gaol* (1898). (Two Rivers Press, 2004)

_____· 'De Profundis' (1905) in *The Works of Oscar Wilde.* (Collins, 1948), pp. 873–957

Periodicals and Newspapers

Annual Register
Gentleman's Magazine
Harmworth's Magazine
Morning Chronicle
Strand Magazine
Spectator
Times Digital Archive

Secondary Sources
Books

Andrews, William. *Bygone Lincolnshire.* (Brown, 1891)

Appignanesi, Lisa. *Mad, Bad and Sad: A History of Women and the Mind Doctors from 1800 to the Present.* (Virago Press, 2008)

Aspinall, Arthur. *Lord Brougham and the Whig Party.* (Archon Books, 1972)

Backsheider, Paula R. *Daniel Defoe: His Life*. (John Hopkins University Press, 1989)

Bate, Walter Jackson. *Samuel Johnson*. (Hogarth Press, 1984)

Birkenhead, Earl of. *Famous Trials*. (Hutchinson, 1911)

Birkett, Sir Norman. *The Newgate Calendar*. (Folio Society, 1951)

Boulton, William B. *The Amusements of Old London*. (John C Nimmo, 1901)

Cashman, D. B. *The Life of Michael Davitt, Founder of the National Land League*. (Harper, 1904)

Cole, G. D. H. *Chartist Portraits*. (Macmillan, 1965)

Cyriax, Oliver. *The Penguin Encyclopaedia of Crime*. (Penguin, 1996)

Delany, Paul. *George Gissing: A Life*. (Phoenix, 2008)

Denning, Lord. *Landmarks in the Law*. (Butterworths, 1984)

Diamond, Michael. *Victorian Sensation*. (Anthem Press, 2004)

Foss, Edward. *A Biographical Dictionary of the Judges of England*. (John Murray, 1870)

Ffrench, Yvonne and Sir John Squire. *News from the Past, 1805–1887: The Autobiography of the Nineteenth Century*. (Gollancz, 1940)

Gatrell, Vic. *City of Laughter: Sex and Satire in Eighteenth Century London*. (Atlantic Books, 2006)

Gibbs, Lewis. *Sheridan*. (J. M. Dent, 1947)

Gibson, James. *Thomas Hardy: A Literary Life*. (St Martin's Press, 1996)

Goldman, Paul. *Victorian Illustrated Books 1850–1870*. (British Museum, 1994)

Grovier, Kelly. *The Gaol: The Story of Newgate*. (John Murray, 2008)

Grundy, Isobel. *Lady Mary Wortley Montagu*. (Oxford University Press, 1999)

Halliday, Stephen. *Newgate, London's Prototype of Hell*. (Sutton, 2006)

Halsband, Robert, ed. *The Complete Letters of Lady Mary Wortley Montagu*. (Oxford University Press, 1966)

Hay, Daisy. *Young Romantics*. (Bloomsbury, 2010)

Hayward, A. *Dr Johnson's Mrs Thrale*. (T. N. Foulis, 1910)

Hibbert, Christopher. *George III: A Personal History*. (Penguin, 1999)

Hickey, D. J. and J. E. Doherty. *A New Dictionary of Irish History from 1800*. (Gill and Macmillan, 2005)

Hill, Christopher. *The Century of Revolution 1603–1714*. (Norton, 1961)

Holmes, Richard. *Dr Johnson and Mr Savage*. (Hodder and Stoughton, 1993)

Howes, Christopher. *How We Saw It: 150 Years of The Daily Telegraph*. (Ebury Press, 2005)

Ingrams, Richard. *The Life and Adventures of William Cobbett*. (Harper, 2006)

James, Louis. *Print and the People 1819–1851*. (Peregrine, 1776)

Lawrence, Frederick. *The Life of Henry Fielding*. (Arthur Hall, Virtue & Co., 1855)

Lewis, D. B. and Charles Lee. *The Stuffed Owl: An Anthology of Bad Verse*. (J. M. Dent, 1930)

Lindsay, David W., ed. *English Poetry 1700–1780*. (J. M. Dent, 1974)

Lucas, E. V. *The Life of Charles Lamb*. (Methuen, 1910)

McNair, Arnold Duncan. *Dr Johnson and the Law*. (Cambridge University Press, 1948)

Makower, S. V. *Richard Savage: A Mystery in Biography*. (1909)

North, Eric M. *Early Methodist Philanthropy*. (Methodist Book Concern, 1914)

Paley, Ruth and Simon Fowler. *Family Skeletons*. (National Archives, 2005)

Papi, Giacomo. *Under Arrest*. (Granta Books, 2006)

Porter, Roy. *Madness: A Brief History*. (Oxford University Press, 2002)

———. *Enlightenment*. (Penguin, 2000)

Rosie, George. *Curious Scotland*. (Granta Books, 2004)

Roughead, William. *The Fatal Countess*. (W. Green, 1924)

Rutherford, Sarah. *The Victorian Asylum*. (Shire, 2008)

Shpayer-Makov, Haia. *The Ascent of the Detective*. (Oxford University Press, 2011)

Sweet, Matthew. *Inventing the Victorians*. (Faber, 2001)

Thornbury, G. W. and E. Walford. *Old and New London*. (Cassell, Petter and Galpin, 1892)

Timbs, John. *Clubs and Club Life in London*. (Chatto and Windus, 1899)

Tomalin, Claire. *Jane Austen: A Life*. (Penguin, 1998)

Tracy, Clarence, ed. *The Poetical Works of Richard Savage*. (Cambridge University Press, 1962)

Tromans, Nicholas. *Richard Dadd: The Artist and the Asylum*. (Tate, 2011)

Tucker, George Holbert. *A History of Jane Austen's Family*. (Sutton, 1998)

Turberville, A. S. *English Men and Manners in the Eighteenth Century*. (Oxford University Press, 1960)

Vallance, Edward. *A Radical History of Britain*. (Abacus, 2009)

Vicinus, Martha, ed. *A Widening Sphere: Changing Roles of Victorian Women*. (Indiana University Press, 1977)

Wharton, Grace and Philip. *The Wits and Beaux of Society*. (James Hogg, 1860)

Articles in Journals and Newspapers/Contributions to Books

Carnocan, W. B. 'The Literature of Confinement' in *The Oxford History of the Prison*, edited by Morris, Norval and Rothman. (Oxford University Press, 1998), pp. 381–406

Colley, Linda. 'Great Writs.' *Times Literary Supplement*. 17 December 2010, pp. 3–4

Irwin, Robert. 'Darkness after the Sun.' *Times Literary Supplement*. 14 October 2011, p. 7

Kureishi, Hanif. 'Reasons to Love Crazy Humanity.' *Independent*. 7 October 2011, p. 28

Murphy, Elaine. 'The Mad-House Keepers of East London.' *History Today* 51: 9 (2001), pp. 29–36

Orwell, George. 'George Gissing' in *The Collected Essays, Journalism and Letters*, vol. 4 (1945–1950). (Penguin, 1970), pp. 485–93

Tomalin, Claire. 'Both a Saint and a Sinner.' *Independent*. 30 September 2011, pp. 22–3

Tyte, Kate. 'For the Criminally Insane.' *Ancestors*. January 2009, pp. 46–50

Websites

Commons Sittings in the 19th Century. http://hansard.millbanksystems.com/commons

Old Bailey Sessions Papers. www.oldbaileyonline.org

The Dorset Page. www.thedorsetpage.com

Newspapers and Periodicals

Annual Register
Daily Chronicle
Daily Graphic
Freeman's Journal
Household Narrative
Illustrated Police News
Independent
Northern Star
Pall Mall Gazette
Times